AWFS

FRESH WOOD DESIGN BOOK

FINISHED WORKS FROM WOODWORKING'S NEXT GENERATION

AWFS

FRESH WOOD DESIGN BOOK

FINISHED WORKS FROM WOODWORKING'S NEXT GENERATION

WINNERS & FINALISTS OF THE FRESH WOOD STUDENT COMPETITION
SPONSORED BY THE ASSOCIATION OF WOODWORKING & FURNISHINGS SUPPLIERS®

CEDAR LANE PRESS

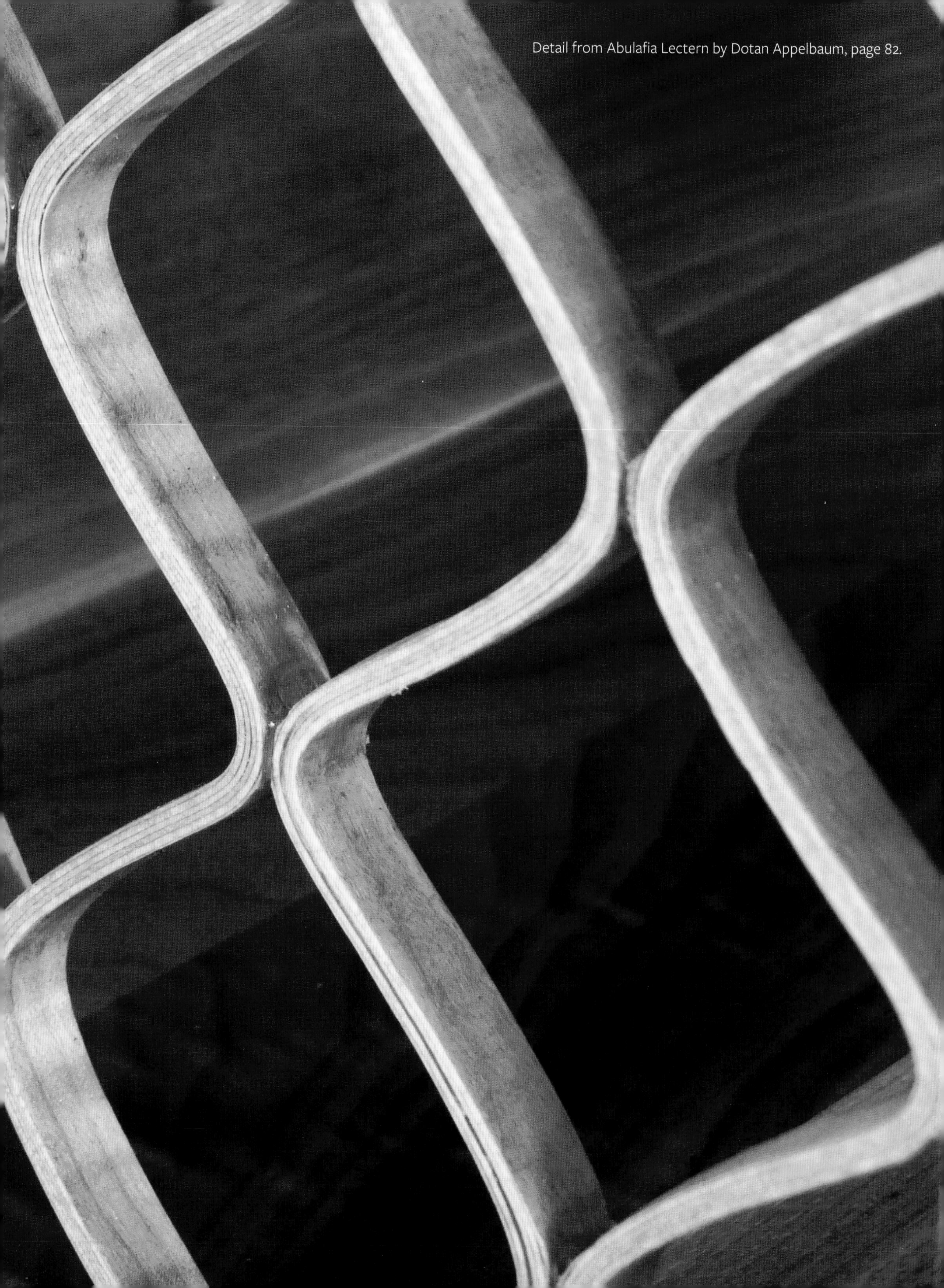

Detail from Abulafia Lectern by Dotan Appelbaum, page 82.

As one of the first Fresh Wood judges and a woodworker with decades of experience, I have been asked many times what makes a good woodworker. Although there are a variety of answers to that question, the projects in this book show what a proven woodworker can do. The elevated level of these entries requires unusual architecture, creative use of materials, and precise execution of joinery to create an exceptional custom appearance that attracts the judges' attention. Participants in this contest can certainly testify as to what it takes to produce these works of art.

It is a continual challenge for woodworking programs to attract students and provide viable classes that reflect the industry. As demonstrated in these pages, the leading programs provide the skills and opportunity for their students to produce championship projects. Competitors in the Fresh Wood contest learn the devotion, skill, and knowledge necessary to craft a project of this caliber. The process is a labor of love, from the initial concept of the piece to the hours of construction utilizing dozens of tools and machines to the storyboard showcasing the unique features of the entry. Finalists then have the opportunity to compare their work with others and to share their accomplishments with industrialists attending the show. One of the most powerful rewards is earning recognition as an exemplary woodworker. There is significant industry demand for such graduates; many will have their pick of career.

> "Anyone involved with Fresh Wood has a better understanding of what it means to be a good woodworker."

The teachers and administrators helping each student also give much to the competition. These educators devote hours to working with the students, mostly beyond normal classroom time. This dedication and teamwork is essential to producing a championship piece. Over the years, I've seen an impressive amount of devotion from both students and educators; this clearly contributes to Fresh Wood's reputation as the number one student woodworking competition in the nation.

The Fresh Wood contest has much to offer. Students, teachers, and school administrators all earn a reputation by participating. Schools and woodworking programs gain exposure and name recognition among potential students and the industry. Attendees have a large pool of candidates to interview for their company's openings; in many cases, this leads directly to filling a position with a qualified woodworker. Even non-industry individuals who view the projects benefit via the experience of seeing woodworking as they never have before. One thing is certain; anyone involved with Fresh Wood has a better understanding of what it means to be a good woodworker.

Duane Griffiths

Duane Griffiths,
Fresh Wood Committee Chair

47

82

112

65

96

132

40

CONTENTS

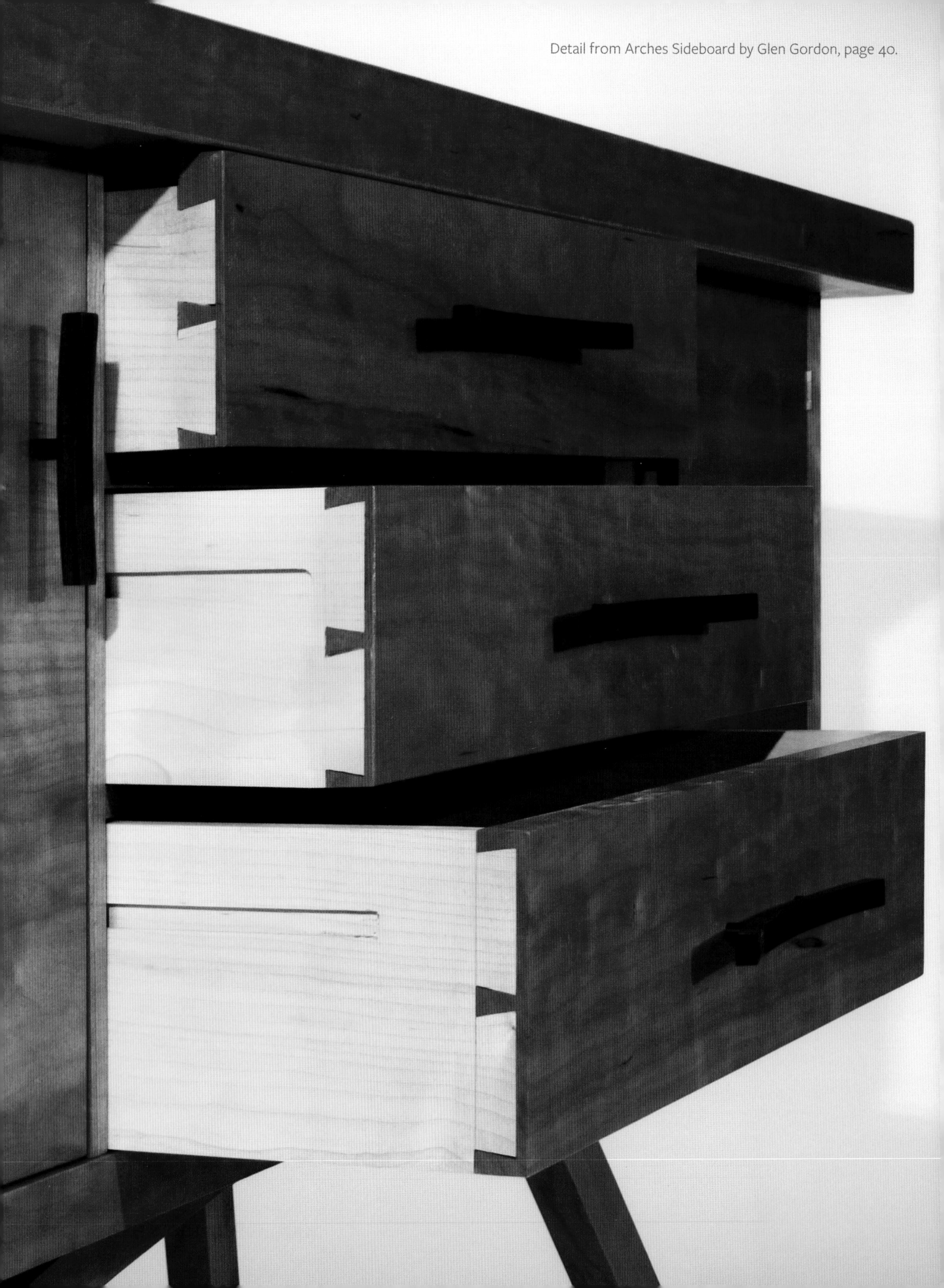

Detail from Arches Sideboard by Glen Gordon, page 40.

Sponsored by the Association of Woodworking & Furnishings Suppliers® (AWFS®), Fresh Wood is a competition for woodworking students who are enrolled in accredited high school and post-secondary schools in the United States and Canada. The competition was created as a vehicle for students to showcase their skills and abilities in wood; to introduce them to the industry as future artists, designers, and woodworkers; and to open career opportunities in the industry through new contacts and relationships

> **"Fresh Wood was created for students to showcase their skill and abilities in wood, to introduce them as future woodworkers, designers, and artists, and to open career opportunities in the industry."**

developed by participating in the event. It is the hope of AWFS® that each student who participates in Fresh Wood leaves inspired, motivated, and a little more prepared for the next step in their woodworking education, or confident enough to pursue other personal or career dreams. For some, the benefit of Fresh Wood is the inaugural experience of participating in a juried exhibition or the opportunity to travel and attend a national industry trade show. In the end, Fresh Wood demonstrates the relevance of the wood manufacturing industry and the potential career opportunities in design, technology, manufacturing, production, management, sales, and countless other capacities.

For the Fresh Wood competition, the students are separated into two groups based on education level, high school and post-secondary, and are encouraged to submit a wide range of work that encompasses innovative, traditional, and manufacturable furniture projects. The entries are separated into six different categories: case goods, seating, tables, design for production, open, and a special theme that varies each year. All the projects must be designed and built in a specified timeframe leading up to the AWFS®Fair, the biennial event owned and operated by AWFS® in Las Vegas, NV. Fresh Wood is free to enter, and AWFS® covers the cost to ship the contending entries to and from the AWFS®Fair, as well as to bring the finalists and their teachers to show.

Judging is done by a panel of professionals representing a range of sectors in the furnishing and woodworking industry, such as design, education, manufacturing, and the woodworking press. In addition to the judges featured in this volume, past panel members have included Gary Rogowski, Marc Spagnuolo, Torben Helshoj, Marc Adams, Paul Epp, Darrell Peart, and many more industry leaders. All entries are reviewed by the judges prior to the AWFS®Fair to determine the finalists that will travel and exhibit at the show. While reviewing the entries, the judges reserve the right to reassign a project to a different category if deemed appropriate. The judges then score each project in areas such as design innovation, quality

The original Best of Show trophy, designed by Sam Maloof, was presented through 2013.

INTRODUCTION

of execution, craftsmanship, functionality, construction, and aesthetics. During the final round of judging at the AWFS®Fair, Fresh Wood judges inspect and interact with the furniture to decide a winner in each category. Throughout the entire process, the student information remains anonymous to the judging panel. Beyond the project, finalists can also earn an additional point if the presentation board highlighting the information about the project and the builder is

JUDGING CRITERIA:

1. Design innovation on original pieces; quality of execution of a known style or variation.
2. Craftsmanship of the piece: construction quality, material choice and use, detailing, sanding quality, and finishing quality.
3. Functionality, stability, comfort, and, if applicable, manufacturability and marketability.
4. Construction techniques: appropriateness of the techniques used, joinery, lamination veneering, or upholstery.
5. Aesthetics: scale, proportion, balance, rhythm, emphasis, and unity.

properly completed per the competition's instructions.

When the smoke clears and the winners have been selected, cash prizes are awarded for first place and second place in each category and at each school level. There are also two top prizes awarded: People's Choice and Best of Show. The People's Choice award is selected by the attendees of the AWFS®Fair and the winner receives a cash prize. For the Best of Show award, the judges select the overall winner who not only receives

a cash prize, but also a distinctive, handcrafted trophy. The original Fresh Wood Best of Show trophy was made by Sam Maloof and, after his passing, Sam Maloof Woodworker, Inc. However, starting in 2015, AWFS® began the tradition of selecting a different woodworker each year to create a unique trophy. For the years covered in this volume, Garry Knox created trophy in 2017; Judson Beaumont in 2019; and Scott Grove in 2021. We're looking forward to seeing the trophy created for the 2023 competition.

The 2017 Best of Show trophy was created by Gary Knox.

About AWFS® and the AWFS®Fair

The Association of Woodworking & Furnishings Suppliers® (AWFS®) was founded in 1911 and is the largest national trade association in the United States representing companies that supply the home and commercial furnishing industry. AWFS® has

an international membership that includes manufacturers and distributors of machinery, hardware, plastics, and other supplies to furniture and cabinet manufacturers, and custom woodworkers.

One of the Association's key objectives is to encourage woodworking education and foster the links between industry and educational organizations. As part of this initiative, AWFS® launched the Student Design Contest, Fresh Wood, in 1999. Other substantial education initiatives include relationships with SkillsUSA California and Woodwork Career Alliance (WCA). SkillsUSA is one of the largest Career and Technical Education student organizations in the nation and emphasizes trade-specific and leadership skill training. The result is the development of students into well-prepared, professional members of the workforce and future leaders in their chosen industries. The Woodwork Career Alliance develops the wood manufacturing

Judson Beaumont's 2019 Best of Show trophy, based on his iconic Apple Cabinet.

skill standards and continually seeks to improve the skill certification program for the industry.

The Fresh Wood competition takes place biennially to correspond with the AWFS®Fair, the official AWFS® trade event held during odd-numbered years in the popular destination of Las Vegas, NV. The AWFS®Fair has become a critical hub for international commerce in the woodworking industry, and brings together the entire home and commercial furnishings industry to buy and sell the latest products and services related to the wood and home furnishings markets. Those attending the AWFS®Fair see firsthand

The 2021 Best of Show trophy was from Scott Grove.

what's new in the industry, improve their knowledge through a wide variety of seminars and demonstrations, and expand their network. Ultimately, they walk away from the event with the ideas, advice, know-how, and connections that will improve their operations and profit.

As an essential component of the AWFS®Fair, the Fresh Wood contest and the exhibition of the selected finalists helps re-shape outdated perceptions of the career opportunities and skill levels in the woodworking industry. It is important for school programs to reflect the changes and advancements caused by evolving technology and a global economy, as well as bring an awareness of the many job openings offering competitive

> **"Those attending the AWFS®Fair leave the event with the ideas, advice, know-how, and connections that will improve their woodworking and wood-related operations."**

salaries for skilled workers in a wide range of career paths. These paths include high-tech machinery operation and repair, computer-controlled machinery operators, sales, international trade, teaching and education, forestry, milling, hardware, machinery and product design, as well as research and development related to coatings, finishings, and innovative wood products that combine with metals, plastics, and solid surfaces. In the end, the Fresh Wood Design Contest at the AWFS®Fair is an excellent way to see first-hand the skills, passion, and vision of the woodworking industry's next generation.

THE FRESH WOOD JUDGES

Jena Hall | 2017
Jena Hall Designs

Jena is an iconic designer and business woman with groundbreaking achievements in the home furnishings and design industry. Her nationally syndicated column for *New York Newsday* and the *Chicago Tribune* ran in over 400 newspapers for 10 years.

Tom McKenna | 2017
Taunton Press

Tom has loved woodworking since he took a basics class during freshman year of high school on Long Island. Now group editorial director for three magazines at Taunton Press, Tom was also the editor of *Fine Woodworking* from 2013 to 2020.

Christopher Poehlmann | 2017
CP Lighting

Chris designs and manufactures furniture, lighting, and other objects of use that walk a willfully blurry line between craft, sculpture, and design. Since 1989, his work has been widely published internationally and exhibited in galleries, museums, and shows.

Mei-yen Shipek | 2017
Autodesk Technology Centers

With a Studio Furniture degree from California College of the Arts, Mei-yen worked at U.C. Berkeley's College of Environmental Design, where she helped set up their digital fabrication lab, created workshop curriculums, and taught CNC.

Scott Vasey | 2017
Advanced Fixtures, Inc.

Scott completed his Masters in Technology at Pittsburg State University while serving as a teaching assistant for the wood technology department. He became interested in woodworking through high school courses and was a Finalist in 2007's Fresh Wood.

Bob Barone | 2019
Precision Drive Systems

Bob is a woodworker and guitar maker in Charlotte, NC. He has owned and operated an architectural millwork company, and has extensive experience in wood, plastic, and engineered composite manufacturing applications.

THE FRESH WOOD JUDGES

Judson Beaumont | 2019
Straight Line Design Inc.

Judson, of Vancouver, BC, Canada, made furniture that was recognized for its unique, creative, and sculptural style. His zany and playful pieces are a testament to his motto, "Take a crazy idea and make it happen."

Scott Grove | 2019
ImagineGrove Woodworking

Scott, of Canandaigua, NY, is an artist, sculptor, and furniture maker known for his advanced woodworking techniques. He lectures and teaches internationally and has been featured in many publications.

Wendy Maruyama | 2019
Bread & Salt

Wendy, a renowned furniture maker and artist from San Diego, CA, led the furniture and woodworking program at San Diego State University from 1989 to 2014. Her work has been exhibited nationally for four decades.

Jim Wellever | 2019
Bridgetown Cabinet Works

Jim, a master cabinetmaker, was head of the cabinetmaking and millwork program and Director of the Midwest Advanced Woodworking Technology Center at Michigan Career & Technical Institute from 2000 to 2020.

Harold Greene | 2021
Harold Greene Handmade Furnishings

Harold is a custom furniture artisan based in California who has specialized in truly memorable furniture designs since 1978. His work has been featured nationally in galleries, museums, and television.

Alan Harp | 2021
Alan Harp Design

Alan has been in furniture design and product development for over 30 years. He taught furniture design at Georgia Tech and was involved in a variety of research projects related to CNC manufacturing and product design.

Taryn Schwartz | 2021
Ballard Designs

Taryn is a product design manager for Ballard Designs in Atlanta, GA. In addition to designing furniture there, Taryn has created watercolor designs used on dinnerware, bedding, and more.

2021

2019

2017

TOP AWARDS

This section showcases the two stand-out projects from each year. To win Best of Show, an entry must be defined by the judges as the best representation of woodworking design and craftsmanship out of all projects from that year. People's Choice is determined by fair attendees, who vote for their favorite. Both awards come with a cash prize; Best of Show winners also receive a specially crafted trophy.

SIDEBOARD WITH A VOID

JINSOO KIM

CENTER FOR FURNITURE CRAFTSMANSHIP | INSTRUCTOR: TIM ROUSSEAU

For more on this project, see page 34.

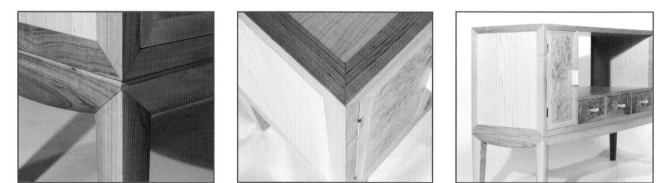

THE NEST

MOHAMMED AL-YASEEN

LINCOLN EAST HIGH SCHOOL | INSTRUCTOR: JON HEITHOLD

For more on this project, see page 96.

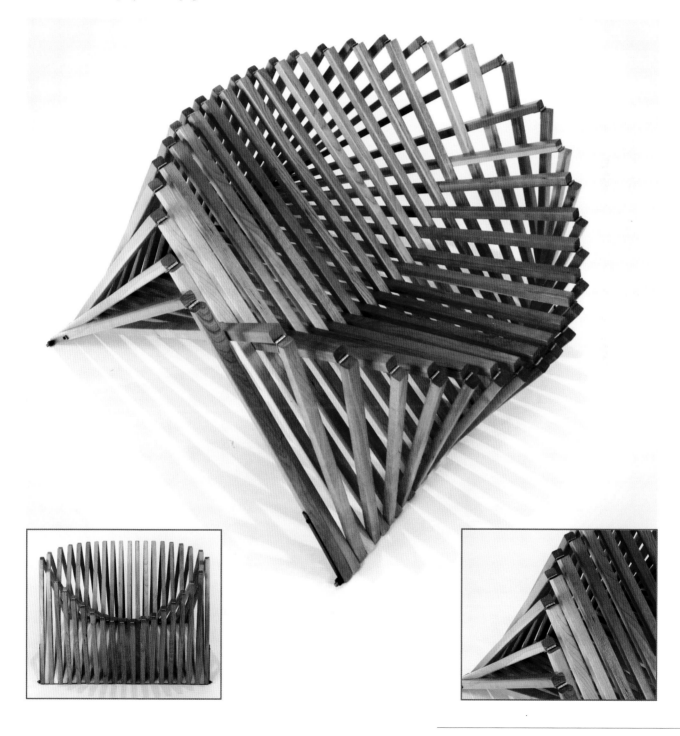

NAUTICAL MARQUETRY TABLE

NICHOLAS MARALDO

THE FURNITURE INSTITUTE OF MASSACHUSETTS | INSTRUCTOR: PHILIP C. LOWE

For more on this project, see page 166.

HARD NINETY

COLE DANIELS

ROLLA TECHNICAL INSTITUTE | INSTRUCTOR: ROBERT STUDDARD

For more on this project, see page 135.

AZULEJOS TABLE

CODY CAMPANIE

SEATTLE CENTRAL COLLEGE | INSTRUCTOR: JEFFREY WASSERMAN

For more on this project, see page 168.

MUSICALLY INCLINED
SARAH PROVARD

WEST JORDAN HIGH SCHOOL | INSTRUCTOR: RICHARD MINOR JR.

For more on this project, see page 28.

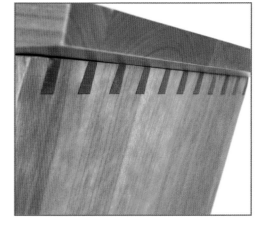

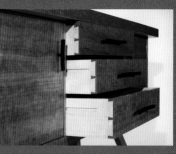

HIGH SCHOOL

⚑ FIRST PLACE

⚑ SECOND PLACE

⚑ FINALIST

POST-SECONDARY

⚑ FIRST PLACE

⚑ SECOND PLACE

⚑ HONORABLE MENTION

⚑ FINALIST

CASE GOODS

The case goods category includes projects such as bed frames, shelving and storage systems, bureaus, dressers, desks, chests, and cabinets. Choice of materials, construction methods, and joinery are considered during judging.

JUKEBOX
DAKOTA KELLEY

ROLLA TECHNICAL INSTITUTE | INSTRUCTOR: ROBERT STUDDARD

What was your inspiration for this piece?

This piece is a retirement gift for our longtime superintendent. He is an avid music lover; it made perfect sense to incorporate modern Bluetooth equipment into a one-of-a-kind piece of furniture.

What were your project goals?

I wanted the uniqueness of the jukebox without all the typical flashiness. I also wanted to have a spot for the record player on top and a drawer to hold all the Bluetooth components and speakers. The bottom drawer is set up to hold vinyl records and other music sources.

What challenges did you encounter?

The biggest challenge was the curved top, specifically cutting the front and back curve and then routing the grooves to accept the curved veneer panel. We dry-fit everything first and then made sure to have everything ready and plenty of hands to help hold things in place. The inset drawers were also a challenge. It took a lot of time to get them all aligned.

Did you use any special equipment or software?

I used AutoCAD software to design the curve for the top. I then used a post processor and sent it to our Weeke CNC router where woodWOP cut the curves and the grooves for the KerfKore. I was able to utilize a local millwork company's 100-year-old dovetail machine to make the dovetail drawers.

DIMENSIONS: 60″ H x 36″ W x 24″ D
WEIGHT: 200 lb.
MATERIALS: Mahogany, maple, KerfKore bending plywood
FINISH: ML Campbell stain, vinyl sealer, and satin Magnalac

OOPS! I BROKE IT.

KAILAN WEIDNER

MUSTANG HIGH SCHOOL | INSTRUCTOR: MIKE McGARRY

2019
1ST
PLACE

What was your inspiration?

This project is based on a cabinet I found pictures of online. I made some intentional minor adjustments out of preference, but mostly stuck to that project.

What were your project goals? Did you use any unique construction methods?

One personal goal of mine is to never use stain, because I just prefer the look of the natural wood. One of the most interesting parts of this project is the sides, which are made of three sheets of plywood, the outmost being walnut, which we glued around a mold designed to get the desired curve.

What challenges did you encounter?

One big challenge was creating the crack in the middle. To do this, I would have to cut the angles in the wood as I went up the crack and find different, creative ways to attach them to the rest of the project. I could not stick completely to the plans, because the angles I cut were always slightly off from the plans, which would throw off the rest of the plans and require adjustments.

DIMENSIONS: 67″ H x 36″ W x 20.5″ D

WEIGHT: 200 lb.

MATERIALS: Walnut (solid, plywood), maple

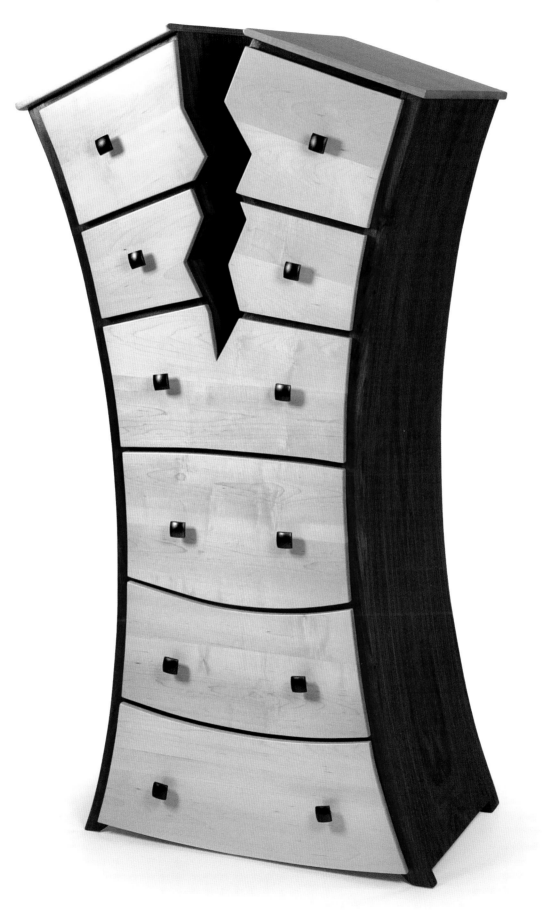

MUSICALLY INCLINED
SARAH PROVARD

WEST JORDAN HIGH SCHOOL | INSTRUCTOR: RICHARD MINOR JR.

2017 1ST PLACE

What was your inspiration for this piece?

When I was trying to select a senior project, I decided to do something with the things that I love most in this world: wood and music. I realized that music and woodworking don't typically go together, so I decided to throw in a little curve to show that I can be different, love both things, and be myself.

What were your project goals? Did you use any unique construction methods?

The main goal was to show my love for both music and wood and also to make people just stand back and say "Wow!"

What challenges did you encounter?

Some of the challenges I had while I was building my project were bending the project, figuring out how to connect the CNC with the laser, figuring out the angles for the keys (each is different), and making all of the detail in the project look stunning.

Did you use any special equipment or software?

At the beginning of this school year, my wood shop gathered enough money to buy a laser; my wood shop teacher and I ended up learning how to use it together. It made the details on the front of my project much easier. The compass spokeshave was a new tool for me; I used it to make the handles smooth.

DIMENSIONS: 66″ H x 48.5″ W x 21″ D

WEIGHT: 201 lb.

MATERIALS: Cherry, hard maple, poplar, aromatic red cedar, cocobolo, Caesalpinia ebano, rosewood, Madagascar rosewood

FINISH: Chemcraft

WALNUT ENTERTAINMENT CREDENZA

FERNANDO CANTU PIRELLI

SAN JACINTO HIGH SCHOOL | INSTRUCTOR: ROY CASTILLO

BRAVO TO TEACHERS 2021

2021 2ND PLACE

What were your project goals?

My project goals were to design and build a functional, aesthetically pleasing, solidly built credenza for my family's house. This walnut credenza was designed to match existing pieces in my home made by members of my family.

What challenges did you encounter?

One challenge was trying to preserve the cove and the small hard lines on the corners of the top while sanding. It was also critical to preserve the roundover on the top's edges. Patience and perseverance were helpful, as were a few shims for the doors and some custom-made sanding and clamping blocks for the molding. Other challenges included matching the grain for my two door panels, getting the wire mesh cut and glued in evenly, and accurately measuring and installing the drop-down door chain length.

Did you use any special equipment or software?

I used a line-boring machine for the adjustable shelf on the inside of the cabinet and a pocket-hole machine for the top frame joinery. Making the cove cut for the molding on the table saw was also new to me.

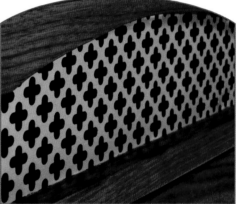

DIMENSIONS: 34″ H x 42″ W x 22″ D
WEIGHT: 210 lb.
MATERIALS: Walnut
FINISH: Boiled linseed oil, tung oil, Watco walnut Danish oil, dark walnut stain (to tint sapwood), beeswax

ZIG-ZAG CORNER CABINET TV STAND

GARRETT VISSCHER

FREMONT HIGH SCHOOL | INSTRUCTOR: RICK TANK

2019
2ND
PLACE

What was your inspiration for this piece?

As I was watching TV thinking about what I might want to build in woodshop class that year, I glanced down at our old, beat-up oak TV stand and decided I wanted to build a beautiful TV cabinet that my parents could have in their home for the rest of their lives.

What were your project goals?
Did you use any unique construction methods?

My goal for this project was to have a very unique design with a good flow and color contrast. I spent quite a few days just thinking of how I wanted it to look, then sketching it out over and over again until the design looked perfect.

DIMENSIONS: 30″ H x 50″ W x 26″ D
WEIGHT: 60 lb.
MATERIALS: Hard maple, black walnut, plywood, hardboard, maple plywood
FINISH: Clear semi-gloss lacquer

What challenges did you encounter?

I encountered a problem when I was trying to glue two 22.5° angles together to make the legs on my project. Because both edges were just butt joints, when I applied pressure, the two boards slipped and wouldn't align. That was when I realized I needed to add some type of joinery to the legs so that when I glued them, they would be aligned. I decided to use a spline joint; not only did this help the boards align perfectly and make gluing much, much easier, it also added a ton of strength that will help with expansion and contraction. Another challenge I faced was to make sure every angle was perfect. I did this by paying really close attention to detail and taking my time when cutting angles.

SYMPHONY OF CONTRAST

KYLE HASSETT

DALE JACKSON CAREER CENTER | INSTRUCTOR: JOSEPH DAVIS

2017
2ND
PLACE

What was your inspiration for this piece?

My inspiration for this project was Japanese carpentry and woodworking. I utilized the curves of traditional Japanese design, and used few screws in the construction. The contrast of the walnut and ash made the handles stand out and also brought the whole dresser together.

What were your project goals?
Did you use any unique construction methods?

I wanted the project to be an unusual piece—something you'd never seen before. I made a jig to create the handles, and also used a steamer to bend them. I used EnRoute CNC software to make a rapid texture design on the side panels.

What challenges did you encounter?

I faced some challenges with the handles. I broke a few and realized that the grain has to be very straight.

DIMENSIONS: 60" H x 45" W x 20" D

WEIGHT: 300 lb.

MATERIALS: Walnut, ash

FINISH: Pre-catalyzed lacquer

HERITAGE PROTECTED

TYLOR GIRARD

DAKOTA HIGH SCHOOL | INSTRUCTOR: CHAD CAMPAU

What was your inspiration for this piece?

Hunting is a rite of passage in my family and I wanted to create something that honors our heritage as well as being functional. The detailed raised panels in the cabinet depict images that evoke the feeling of late fall in upper Michigan. The shotgun carousel has a smooth post, just like a shotgun barrel. At the top of the post is a turned shotgun shell with carved ridges. The other carousel, for rifles, has rifling on the post and a turned rifle shell on top. The upper side cabinets are for a crossbow and compound bow.

What challenges did you encounter?

Learning the MasterCAM software for the raised panels was difficult and time consuming. I used a lathe to create the two different shells atop the gun carousels; learning how to place the tool correctly on the material without the material pulling the cutting edge across the surface was difficult. The rifling of the post was completed using a Legacy machine; it was challenging to learn proper setup for the post.

DIMENSIONS: 81″ H x 66″ W x 33″ D

WEIGHT: 425 lb.

MATERIALS: Cherry, maple, plywood (top and bottom), glass

FINISH: Spar lacquer

SIDEBOARD WITH A VOID

JINSOO KIM

CENTER FOR FURNITURE CRAFTSMANSHIP | INSTRUCTOR: TIM ROUSSEAU

What was your inspiration for this piece?
This project is inspired by the traditional Korean sideboard.

What were your project goals?
Did you use any unique construction methods?
My goal was to modernize this piece of Korean traditional furniture in terms of both design and construction technique. One unique part of this piece is the void. The user completes the design of the sideboard by filling the void with their own objects according to their own ideas. Traditional Korean miter joints were an important factor of the design. They make a more organic connection than butt joints. The connection between the rails and panels of the top case show-faces are flush joints. This makes the big, complicated case look like one simple piece.

What challenges did you encounter?
To make this piece structurally strong but lightweight, I made three types of boards to suit different purposes. The top is 1″ thick, but kept light with a composition of maple veneer, plywood, and cardboard honeycomb core. Conventional composition of veneer and a thin plywood core made the sides of the top case. The doors were made from a slab of glued-up pine strips sandwiched between birdseye maple veneer. Another challenge was creating the flush connection between the four miter-joint rails and the boards.

Did you use any special equipment or software?
For verification of size and proportion, I created a design using the Rhino program, and then made a 1:1 cardboard mockup model. After finalizing the design, I drew 2D drawings for the construction in the AutoCAD program and extracted 3D data from the modeling geometry in the Rhino program.

DIMENSIONS: 32″ H x 50″ W x 17″ D
WEIGHT: 100 lb.
MATERIALS: Maple, birdseye maple, poplar, pine, plywood, cardboard honeycomb core
FINISH: Osmo Polyx-oil, shellac

CABINET END TABLE

CHRISTOPHER MERCHANT

CENTER FOR FURNITURE CRAFTSMANSHIP | INSTRUCTOR: ALED LEWIS

2019
1ST
PLACE

What were your project goals?
Did you use any unique construction methods?

This piece was an exploration of case piece construction. All the components adhere to an angled taper, so standard case construction had to be rethought with these particular needs in mind. The most unique design element was the tapered bevel that frames the drawers and doors on the front of the piece. This bevel adds considerable complexity and visual interest because it introduces a subtle rake to the front plane of the case even though the sides are rectilinear.

What challenges did you encounter?

The most challenging part of this design was in hinging the doors; the bottom outside corners of the doors pivot into the cavity of the cabinet when the doors open. I solved this problem by creating my own hinge system out of solid brass. I learned to solder and created a set of knife hinges for the tops of the doors. For the bottoms, I turned a 3/8″ brass rod into a 1/8″ pin at the top and let the rod into the bottom of the cabinet. A piece of brass with a 1/8″ hole was positioned on the bottoms of the doors such that the whole door pivoted on an axis between the knife hinge pins and the turned brass pins in the bottom. Complicating this process further was the fact that the doors are slightly tipped back along the plane of the front of the case.

DIMENSIONS: 38″ H x 18″ W x 12″ D
WEIGHT: 75 lb.
MATERIALS: Maple
FINISH: Osmo

ASH CABINET

JOE BROWN

CENTER FOR FURNITURE CRAFTSMANSHIP | INSTRUCTOR: ALED LEWIS

What was your inspiration for this piece?

The inspiration was a cabinet by W. Walker, a student of James Krenov. Walker's cabinet on a stand was a study in grain, with emphasis on horizontal and vertical patterns.

What were your project goals?
Did you use any unique construction methods?

The project goals were to design an elegant, contemporary case piece and highlight a wood with a unique grain pattern.

What challenges did you encounter?

The design having attached legs in lieu of a stand introduced stability issues, which were resolved through the addition of lower stretchers between and among the legs. This addition required floating tenons with a 45° angle. The addition of the stretchers also added complications to the case glue-up, which were resolved by adding two members to the glue-up team and using epoxy; its longer open time allowed for the additional parts. The doors were book-matched, shop-sawn veneer designed with lipping from the same board to provide a solid-wood appearance. Addressing grain on six sides provided a challenge, which was met through a studied approach.

The design called for a top-to-floor line for all legs and all edges. Hinge mortises were cut on an angle to provide a "cabinetmaker's mortise" wherein the line of the 45° angle where the cabinet meets the leg is not interrupted by the mortise or hinge; the hinge sits proud to the line.

DIMENSIONS: 54″ H x 36″ W x 14″ D

WEIGHT: 35 lb.

MATERIALS: Ash (solid, shop-sawn veneer), birch plywood

FINISH: Water-based polyurethane

ARCHES SIDEBOARD

GLEN GORDON

CENTER FOR FURNITURE CRAFTSMANSHIP | INSTRUCTOR: TIM ROUSSEAU

2021
2ND
PLACE

What was your inspiration for this piece?

This piece was inspired by a trestle table with dramatically splayed legs made by Wharton Esherick. The arched stretches were inspired by the form of an arch bridge, which has immense strength and good lines.

What were your project goals?
Did you use any unique construction methods?

The greatest goal was to come up with a joint for the arched leg support that didn't rely on glue. The other primary goal was to make the case with exceptional color and grain matching. This was done by making all of the exposed parts (on the front, top, and sides) from solid wood or shop-sawn veneer taken from a single board.

What challenges did you encounter?

First, achieving the color and grain matching goals required significant planning to conserve the wood available in the one board used. This also meant that I had no spare parts, so any mistakes needed to be corrected. Second, the joint between the arched stretchers and the front to back stretchers in the leg system had to withstand a high-tension load even if the glue joint were to fail. Developing this custom joint—a recessed, mitered lap joint—was a three-day process.

Did you use any special equipment or software?

Much of the case is made using shop-sawn veneer. The veneer was applied to the substrate (MDF) in a vacuum press, which I had not previously used. The arched leg stretchers were steam bent; I had not previously used a steam box or bending straps.

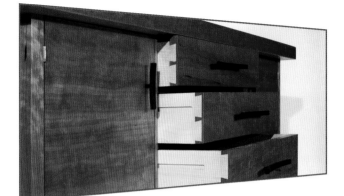

DIMENSIONS: 36″ H x 54″ W x 18″ D

WEIGHT: 60 lb.

MATERIALS: Cherry (solid, shop-sawn veneer), MDF, maple, rosewood, poplar torsion box with cardboard honeycomb

FINISH: Shellac, tung oil

WALNUT JEWELRY CABINET

ZALA OUYANG

NORTH BENNET STREET SCHOOL | INSTRUCTOR: DAN FAIA

2019 2ND PLACE

What was your inspiration for this piece?

I wanted to make a case piece that was small in size, simple in appearance, and complex in construction. I have always liked continuous tambour construction, so I designed the cylinder carcase to incorporate continuous tambour.

What were your project goals?
Did you use any unique construction methods?

This project was intended to teach me the construction of tambour, designing and fitting the top and bottom tracks, veneering, bricking and dovetailing a curved drawer, turning a plate, and turning brass hardware on a regular wood lathe.

What challenges did you encounter?

It was very difficult to assemble the tambour wall, tambour door, and inner veneer wall with the round top and base pieces. Any slight misalignment would cause the tambour door not to function smoothly. This added difficulty to the glue-up process. To solve this problem, I first glued the base pieces to the walls, then made registration marks on the top piece and the walls. I also rehearsed a lot of times until I could align and assemble them within five minutes.

Did you use any special equipment or software?

I made jigs and patterns for the router to make the tracks to hold the tambour wall, door, and inner veneer wall. I also made a jig using benchtop hold-down clamps to hold a ruler for registering the cut lines of the veneered tambour pieces.

DIMENSIONS: 11.5" H x 12" W x 12" D

WEIGHT: 10 lb.

MATERIALS: Walnut (solid, veneer)

FINISH: Epifanes varnish

LI'L DIPPER

MATT GIOVINGO

THE KRENOV SCHOOL | INSTRUCTOR: LAURA MAYS

What was your inspiration for this piece?

I set out to challenge myself and build something that relied on non-square construction with pleasing visual elements in lovely yet difficult pearwood. I was inspired by the beautiful coopered-door cabinets of James Krenov and the traditional methods of construction used in his process.

What were your project goals?
Did you use any unique construction methods?

I wanted to explore asymmetry and curves in design and production using purpose-built planes to achieve the coopered elements. Everything I did in this piece, for me, was a new experience. From doweling the carcase to coopering the doors and making the brass hinges, I set goals to learn as much as I could in a small piece and I feel I succeeded.

What challenges did you encounter?

Pearwood is notorious for showing flaws in construction, especially glue lines. The glue seams of traditional coopering methods using staves would have been very difficult to impossible to hide in such a homogeneous, light material. The challenge of excavating the curved panels was solved by beginning with thick stock, scribing the curves on end grain, and using a table saw by slowly adjusting the height of the blade and the fence to kerf-out material to the scribe lines. A coopering plane was then used to waste away the remaining material down to the line, giving me a precise end result.

DIMENSIONS: 11" H x 24" W x 8" D

WEIGHT: 10 lb.

MATERIALS: Swiss pear (steamed, unsteamed), Monterey cypress, manzanita

FINISH: Shellac

CHEST OF DRAWERS

ALEXANDER TOLINI

HAYWOOD COMMUNITY COLLEGE | INSTRUCTOR: BRIAN WURST

2019
HM
HONORABLE
MENTION

What was your inspiration for this piece?

This chest of drawers takes some inspiration from classic bombe dressers. Ultimately, since the dresser was a present for my mother, I attempted to create a very opulent, yet functional, piece.

What challenges did you encounter?

The most difficult part was getting the edges of the drawer faces to appear as a clean line with equal thickness. This was achieved with lots of careful planing, sanding, and test fitting.

Did you use any special equipment or software?

I made templating jigs to get the drawer faces symmetrical; I designed the piece in SketchUp.

DIMENSIONS: 46″ H x 50″ W x 18″ D
WEIGHT: 300 lb.
MATERIALS: Shop-sawn curly maple veneer, makore (solid, hammered veneer), laminated poplar, maple plywood
FINISH: Arm-R-Seal oil/urethane, EMTECH EM6000 lacquer

MT. ROCKVALE VANITY

TYLER WILLMON

CENTER FOR FURNITURE CRAFTSMANSHIP | INSTRUCTOR: ALED LEWIS

What was your inspiration for this piece?

My wife and I have always shared small homes, but I wanted her to have a space to prepare and unwind from the day. Rockvale is the small, rural town in Tennessee she grew up in, and the mirror "mountain" is a reminder of the hill traversed to visit her childhood home.

What were your project goals?
Did you use any unique construction methods?

The school segment at the time was case pieces, so I wanted to fulfill that, in addition to getting practice making legs. I used a lot of cardboard for making mock-ups to get proportions before spending any unnecessary time milling wood. Making 1:8 scale models proved to be helpful as well.

What challenges did you encounter?

This was my first bent lamination experience. It was pretty straightforward, but took some forethought to ensure the mirror frame lined up with the splay of the legs. Sorting through how to incorporate the mirror also took some head scratching. Initially I was planning on a complex bent lamination that would transition into the back legs. In the end it made the most sense to make the mirror a separate piece, both for ease of transport, and for a more toned-down aesthetic. The brass hardware was the most troublesome. I tried many variations of antiquing, but in the end I figured out how to tone down the brass because I felt the color was most compatible with the white oak.

DIMENSIONS: 56″ H x 36″ W x 15″ D

WEIGHT: 63 lb.

MATERIALS: White oak, mirror

FINISH: Osmo Wood Wax Finish (White, Cognac), Osmo Satin Matte Polyx-Oil

CHERRY BOWFRONT CABINET

JOSHUA STERNS

THE KRENOV SCHOOL | INSTRUCTOR: LAURA MAYS

2017
HM
HONORABLE MENTION

What was your inspiration for this piece?

This project was an attempt to combine traditional Western construction, a hand-cut dovetailed carcase, and frame-and-panel doors and back with Japanese shoji panels in a way that would look natural and harmonious.

What were your project goals?
Did you use any unique construction methods?

I wanted the cabinet to have an effect of simplicity when viewed as a whole, with complexities emerging when one takes a closer look. To achieve the curved shoji panels, I started by constructing flat panels several times thicker than is typical and then shaped them to the curve of the door. Modular design was also a goal, which is why the removable drawer box is fully dovetailed and can be treated as a separate piece of furniture when removed.

What challenges did you encounter?

One of the parameters for this project was that any curves were to be cut out rather than bent or laminated. This necessitated a great deal of hand shaping of the rails for the curved double doors using spokeshaves, card scrapers, and a compass plane. Cutting bridle joints in the curved pieces also presented a challenge. In order to hold the curved pieces at the correct angles on the bandsaw and table saw, I devised a simple jig that can work for infinite curves and angles.

DIMENSIONS: 20.5" H x 15" W x 7.5" D

WEIGHT: 15 lb.

MATERIALS: Cherry, cypress, maple, manzanita

FINISH: Shellac, wax mixed with turpentine and mineral spirits

ROSEWOOD ENTERTAINMENT STAND

ERICA STROM

SELKIRK COLLEGE | INSTRUCTOR: DAVID RINGHEIM

What was your inspiration for this piece?

My teachers encouraged me to work with some curves, and I also wanted to have a project featuring wood and metal. This led me to research vintage styles of furniture, including Mid-Century Modern and Modern. This project was inspired by historical pieces but took a shape of its own as I moved along the design process.

What were your project goals?
Did you use any unique construction methods?

The goal of this project was to build a TV stand for myself that satisfied the requirements of my assignment in a creative and unique way. To achieve the effect of the wood grain running across the top and then cascading down to the floor, I had to produce a bent lamination. Knowing that the laminations were going to have exposed substrate along the edges, I came up with the idea of edging all the panels with copper.

What challenges did you encounter?

I very quickly learned that designing projects with curves takes woodworking to a whole new level. 1/4″ Bendy Ply yielded the tightest radius; I laminated several together to achieve the thicknesses I desired. I then devised a bending form to be used in the vacuum bag press. To achieve the look of the grain flowing across the front and into the left side, I decided to use invisible SOSS hinges. Finding an adhesive for copper was also a challenge. My tests revealed solvent-based contact cement was the best result.

DIMENSIONS: 20″ H x 47″ W x 16″ D
WEIGHT: 40 lb.
MATERIALS: Bendable plywood, MDF, Santos rosewood (veneer), mahogany, copper
FINISH: Spray lacquer

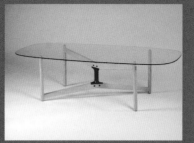

HIGH SCHOOL

POST-SECONDARY

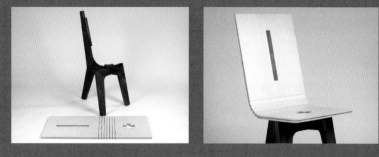
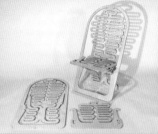

![gear icon]

DESIGN FOR PRODUCTION

Projects in this category are designed to be functional mass-produced items. The focus is on cost-effective machine-reproduceable designs that are also efficient to ship. New in 2021, entries must be CNC-cut from a single sheet of 4×8 plywood. Students must also consider how to successfully market and package their projects.

2021
1ST
PLACE

LUMBAREST

JOSIAH MILES

LINCOLN EAST HIGH SCHOOL | INSTRUCTOR: JON HEITHOLD

What was your inspiration for this piece?

This set of chairs was inspired by the designs of Gregg Fleishman; they are an authentic reproduction of his design as extrapolated from a series of pictures. My intent was two-fold: study the great works of Fleishman and efficiently produce a matched set of chairs from a single sheet of material. I contacted Gregg Fleishman and received his full blessing to produce the chair.

What were your project goals?

The main goal was to maximize the use of one 4x8 sheet of plywood. I had to cut through the sheet, leave some with bridges to the parent piece, and then flush-trim the remaining bridge material to free the chair parts from the original sheet. Ultimately, two chairs were created from one sheet of plywood.

What challenges did you encounter?

Assembly of the chair is a bit of a puzzle; although there may be other ways to assemble the seat to the base, I have a way that works well and is foolproof. Coincidently, this chair is sometimes referred to as "the puzzle chair" by the Fleishman faithful. Easing or rounding over of the edges was also a consideration so the chair could have a more comfortable feel than the original sharp router-cut edges.

Did you use any special equipment or software?

The process focused on the digitizing of some image files into CAD drawings that could be modified in AutoCAD and prepared for nesting in a CAD/CAM code writing software.

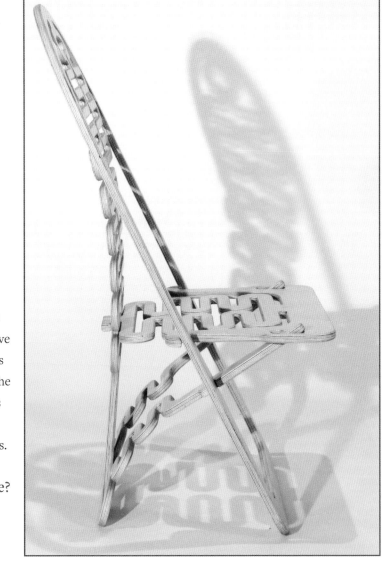

DIMENSIONS: 42" H x 24" W x 24" D

WEIGHT: 30 lb.

MATERIALS: Birch plywood

FINISH: Water-based lacquer

SUPER SCOOT

JACK REZNICH & ETHAN NESS

FRANKFORT HIGH SCHOOL | INSTRUCTOR: DAVID BARRESI

What was your inspiration for this piece?
We wanted to give our families and the new generation a product they could look back and reminisce about. Toys nowadays just aren't built to last, so we decided to change that.

What were your project goals?
We wanted everyone to walk away knowing they were a huge part in creating this unique, colorful, durable, and fun scooter. The second goal was to make a profit.

What challenges did you encounter?
We originally underestimated the wood we needed by half. Another issue we ran into was finding a good way to apply the rubber coat to the wheels. In general, we struggled with our lack of overall experience.

What is the intended market for this product?
Our intended market is the grandparents and parents of 1–3-year-old children.

What considerations were given to the product's production efficiency?
We made the production of our piece efficient by creating all angled pieces at 15° and by using radii for all of the curved pieces. Our product will be able to be shipped in a 15″ x 19″ x 31″ box with some assembly required.

DIMENSIONS: 18″ H x 30″ W x 14″ D

WEIGHT: 9 lb.

MATERIALS: POPLAR

FINISH: Spray paint

THE DADDY CHAIR

CODY WESTERMAN

DEER PARK HIGH SCHOOL | INSTRUCTOR: KEVIN KERNAN

2017
1ST
PLACE

What was your inspiration for this piece?

My inspiration for this piece was to have an Adirondack chair that I could have at my lake cabin; something that I could call my own. I then decided one wouldn't be enough and two would be perfect.

What were your project goals?

The goals were to complete a project that I could be proud of and have a great conversation starter.

What challenges did you encounter?

I did experience design challenges that came during the cutting stage. The CNC table wouldn't cut very well on the right side of the table, but on the left side it cut perfectly.

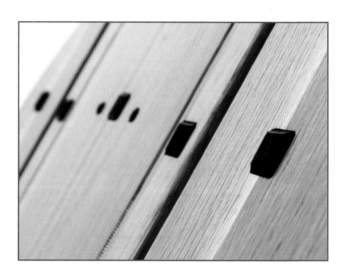

Did you use any special equipment or software?

I utilized SolidWorks and Aspire to design; a Laguna Tools CNC router cut out all the pieces, except for the seat slats (which I ripped on the table saw).

What considerations were given to the product's production efficiency?

Each piece was designed and saved on Aspire and SolidWorks, so within a few hours it could all be cut out on a CNC machine. One could have their own Adirondack chair shipped to their home through freight, unassembled and in their desired wood preference. Buyers could then stain it at home.

DIMENSIONS: 40″ H x 40″ W x 40″ D
WEIGHT: 80 lb.
MATERIALS: White oak, wenge
FINISH: Formby's Furniture Workshop
Traditional Tung Oil Finish

SOME ASSEMBLY REQUIRED

MOHAMMED AL-YASEEN

LINCOLN EAST HIGH SCHOOL | INSTRUCTOR: JON HEITHOLD

2021
2ND
PLACE

What was your inspiration for this piece?

For years in our school's introduction to engineering class, students were challenged to maximize the use of a sheet of cardboard for a chair prototype. Many students commented that the next phase of the design process would be to implement their concepts to a ¾″ x 4′ x 8′ sheet of plywood. There are many slotted chair examples on the market today and one in particular that served as inspiration for this piece is the Luken Mecedora chair.

What were your project goals?

The main goal was to make a functional and comfortable chair for the home office or a dining room. Another goal was to consider the shipping aspect of delivering this item to customers as flat pack furniture that would be simple to assemble and put to use right out of the box.

What challenges did you encounter?

The overall challenge was to maximize the use of the sheet stock to eliminate waste and promote sustainability. Particular attention was paid to the common ergonomic standards that are employed in the design of chairs and people in the seated position. Careful consideration was taken to create subtle lumbar support and an appropriate seat-to-backrest angle. The concept started with sketches, a SketchUp massing study, and then evolved to placing human scale figures in the seated position into the CAD model.

Did you use any special equipment or software?

Design software included SketchUp, SolidWorks, EnRoute, and CNC Controller 12.

DIMENSIONS: 39″ H x 18″ W x 20″ D
WEIGHT: 41 lb.
MATERIALS: Birch plywood

RIOT ARTS GAMING CHAIR
CHANDLER NORTON

REED-CUSTER HIGH SCHOOL | INSTRUCTOR: MARK SMITH

2019
2ND
PLACE

What was your inspiration for this piece?

My inspiration was the Opendesk website's knock-down products and my love of gaming. My teacher had the CAD/CAM 2 class look at a number of different websites to help generate ideas for our project. We have a number of knock-down furniture items sitting around the classroom that helped with the idea as well.

What were your project goals?
Did you use any unique construction methods?

This project was part of my independent study class where I reinforced the skills I learned in my other industrial technology classes. I used an interlocking friction fit joint to hold the chair together. No screws or traditional wood joints were used.

What challenges did you encounter?

I had to redesign the interlocking parts that are near the back and bottom of the chair to maximize stability without using screws. I created a scaled-down version and cut the parts out on our CNC laser. The prototype showed me the design weaknesses that needed to be reworked. The biggest challenge was designing the chair so the interlocking openings were the same width as the parts that would fit down in them.

Did you use any special equipment or software?

I used AutoCAD to design all the parts and MasterCAM to create the toolpaths to run the Thermwood Model 43 CNC router. I also used our Universal Laser to create the prototype.

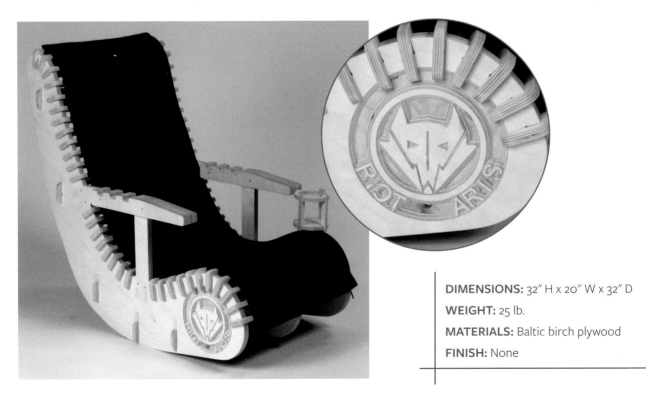

DIMENSIONS: 32″ H x 20″ W x 32″ D

WEIGHT: 25 lb.

MATERIALS: Baltic birch plywood

FINISH: None

AURORA

ELIZABETH MAWALAL

FLETCHER'S MEADOW SECONDARY SCHOOL | INSTRUCTOR: PETER BOECKH

2017
2ND PLACE

What was your inspiration for this piece?

I was inspired by the image of a whale sounding, preparing to dive below the surface, and that moment when her tail would come up out of the water. The very rich appearance, with the silhouette and positive and negative shapes, is intended to be further highlighted by a finish of opaque black or white lacquer. I took the prototype further to present an upgrade with an exotic wood veneer surface, in this case inspired by the aurora borealis.

What challenges did you encounter?

Creating the complex curved form out of foam and using a vacuum table to mimic the commercial process proved to be a lot of work for just a one-off, while lacking the bending power that a commercial hydraulic or vacuum forming system would provide. This was especially apparent when it came time to apply the curly maple veneer. Without access to a large vacuum bag, I had to use contact cement for this step, with less-than-ideal holding power as a result.

Did you use any special equipment or software?

A vacuum table was used.

What considerations were given to the product's production efficiency?

Requiring just six sheets of 1/8″ Baltic birch plus an upholstered seat, the chair could be mass produced very easily once a mold was produced. Template routing would quickly cut out the complex contours, leaving a ready-to-finish edge. Assembly would be simple, allowing for tighter packaging and warehouse space. It remains, however, a complex shape requiring bubble wrap and foam for protection and some packaging volume.

DIMENSIONS: 55″ H x 39″ W x 32″ D
WEIGHT: 65 lb.
MATERIALS: Baltic birch bending plywood, curly maple veneer on phenolic backer

72.5 CHAIR

NATHAN MIKLO & SAMUEL CHRISTIANSON

IOWA STATE UNIVERSITY | INSTRUCTOR: MATTHEW OBBINK

2019
1ST
PLACE

What was your inspiration for this piece?

Our inspiration for this piece came from looking at flat-pack designs that were just not high quality. When you think of handmade, you think of expensive and long lasting. When you think of flat pack, you think of disposable, cheap materials. We wanted to provide an option that bridges the gap between high quality and easy shipping.

What were your project goals?

Our project goal was to create an extremely minimal yet durable chair. We wanted to create a single back piece that would be able to fold flat in a package as well as connect all the legs together.

What challenges did you encounter?

When creating a full bending backrest, we ran into the trouble of being able to perfectly align the pieces that come through the backrest to lock it into place. We were able to create multiple templates from paper along the spine of the back leg to be able to correctly position each of the holes accordingly.

Did you use any special equipment or software?

We used SolidWorks and KeyShot to model and visualize our chair design. We also used laser cutting to create mini models.

DIMENSIONS: 39″ H x 17″ W x 22″ D

WEIGHT: 25 lb.

MATERIALS: Baltic birch plywood, walnut, leather

FINISH: Wipe-on poly, soap varnish

What considerations were given to the product's production efficiency?

Our entire design pulls apart in only three separate pieces that can be CNC machined. All of the parts of the chair lay completely flat to be stored and shipped inside a box or specialized crate.

PUA SIDE TABLE

EVAN BOYLE

CENTER FOR FURNITURE CRAFTSMANSHIP | INSTRUCTOR: ALED LEWIS

2017 1ST PLACE

What was your inspiration for this piece?

This is an original design that is inspired by the beautiful greenery and flowers that are all around us. With blooming flowers, light petals, and colorful, curvy features in mind, this table was designed for function and beauty.

What were your project goals?

This table was specifically designed for a chic Bohemian beach home; I wanted to bring the outside in. My project goal was to design and build a beautiful side table that both resembles and holds flowers. I want to provide the client with a product that memories can be built around for years to come.

What challenges did you encounter?

The top is thin to give a sleek appearance, which is hard to do with turned tenons on the legs that do not go all the way through the top. Because of this, the joinery from the leg to the top is not as deep as I would have preferred. To counter this, I designed the unique stretchers between the legs to add structure and strength to the piece.

Did you use any special equipment or software?

I used a shaper for the underside bevel of the top and a lathe for the legs and stretchers. I made angled drill press jigs to achieve the splay of the legs, as well as the angled joinery of the stretchers.

What considerations were given to the

product's production efficiency?

I designed specific jigs and templates for an expedient build. I have reduced my build time on the table to approximately five hours. The table can ship flat, but it would take a customer who wouldn't mind completing a glue assembly. Even though it can ship flat, I see it more as a fully assembled and boxed item.

DIMENSIONS: 22″ H x 20″ W x 20″ D

WEIGHT: 10 lb.

MATERIALS: Black walnut, glass (top and vase)

FINISH: Clear finish

ARTIST'S DESK
OSAMU SASSA
CENTER FOR FURNITURE CRAFTSMANSHIP | INSTRUCTOR: ALED LEWIS

2019
2ND
PLACE

What was your inspiration for this piece?
The desk floats above the floor, expressed as a cantilevered form at one end. The case component has no front or back, left or right side. It is meant to sit in the middle of or divide a space where the artist can work alone or sit opposite a friend, colleague, or client. A single drawer and a pair of doors can be accessed equally from both sides.

What challenges did you encounter?
Wood movement was especially challenging on this approximately 5 1/2′-long piece. In order to firmly secure the top to the stretcher, threaded steel plates were embedded and mortised into the top prior to glue up.

What is the intended market for this product?
It works particularly well for artists, writers, and creative-minded people. The desk can be used from both sides, welcoming the interaction of two people working across the table to collaborate on ideas.

What considerations were given to the product's production efficiency?
The piece can be put together within five minutes using seven bolts. The three main components have been engineered with embedded steel plates to allow for efficient assembly.

DIMENSIONS: 15″ H x 83″ W x 26″ D
WEIGHT: 55 lb.
MATERIALS: Ash
FINISH: Spray lacquer, super-blonde shellac

5-DAY VALET

CHRIS WESTFALL

UNIVERSITY OF KENTUCKY | INSTRUCTOR: MICHAEL JACOBS

What was your inspiration for this piece?

I was inspired by both wardrobes and valets, and wanted this piece to be a combination of both, allowing for organization of clothes for the work week. When viewed from the bedroom door, you see a tall, slender wooden screen with dots of color from the clothes behind. From this view it is a sculptural piece. The full contents are not visible until you walk to the more private part of the bedroom; it is both functional and private without any doors or drawers, reducing the material needed.

What were your project goals?
Did you use any unique construction methods?

The primary goal for this project was to find the right balance between manufacturing time and joy of assembly once the box arrives on a customer's doorstep. CNC-cut holes precisely align parts, allowing for the act of stitching to be both straightforward and rewarding. Additionally, the signature component is two-ply veneer, with a good face on the front and back. This means that, while less material is being used and shipped, it still has the appearance of a high-quality piece.

What challenges did you encounter?

Finishing a sheet of veneer with 3,200 holes is understandably difficult. To avoid this, I finished both sides of the material before it was cut. The coats of polyurethane seem to act as a glue for keeping the edges clean when cut.

What considerations were given to the product's production efficiency?

Using the CNC mill for its precision capabilities along with traditional wood-cutting tools, the piece was designed to be easily replicated. Also, since the veneer parts are thin, it only takes one pass with the CNC to cut all the way through. The entire piece was designed so that it can fit in a long but narrow box, staying within the bounds of common shipping dimensional restraints.

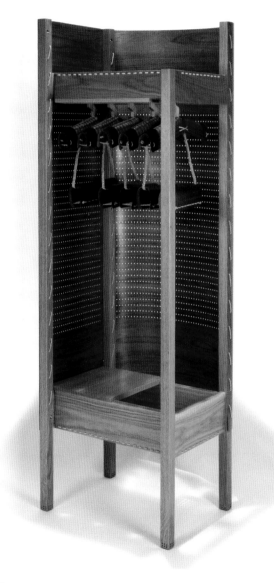

DIMENSIONS: 74″ H x 23.5″ W x 23.5″ D

WEIGHT: 57 lb.

MATERIALS: Walnut (two-ply veneer), white oak

FINISH: Danish oil, Danish oil and polyurethane mix, hand-rubbed polyurethane

MARIPOSA CONVERTIBLE TABLE

HUNG DUONG

JAMES MADISON UNIVERSITY | INSTRUCTOR: KEVIN PHAUP

2019

F

FINALIST

What was your inspiration for this piece?

I noticed a need for better ready-to-assemble (RTA) table designs. Research showed that RTA tables are short-term solutions; the assembly can be difficult, and the average lifespan of a table is well less than what it used to be in the past. The table pays homage to the long-lasting designs of the past, but also embraces modern and minimalist principals from today. I wanted the table to be a common ground to spark conversation with others; it converts from a low-top coffee table to a high-top cafe table.

What were your project goals?

The project goals were to create something with minimal assembly and multiple purposes that could be easily produced, but also still have integrity at an affordable price.

DIMENSIONS: 14″ H x 28″ W x 24″ D
WEIGHT: 35 lb.
MATERIALS: Maple, glass
FINISH: Satin polyurethane

What challenges did you encounter?

Some design challenges that I faced were how to make something easily repeatable without losing form and function, and just if the design itself would work in general. I made about a dozen mini wireframe models before choosing a few to make as full-scale models.

Did you use any special equipment or software?

To create the mortises and tenons, I modeled and 3D-printed jigs to give me precise templates for chiseling.

What is the intended market for this product?

People are moving more now than they once did, and this table would allow for quick assembly and easy transportation while also giving them something made with longevity in mind.

What considerations were given to the product's production efficiency?

This product is unique in that it is a flat, packable RTA table with two table orientations that only requires four screws for assembly. The legs and struts are made out of common and abundant species of wood. The central connector can be milled with a five-axis milling machine or even made out of high-density plastic.

LINDA
GEORGE (RANDY) ZUBIETA
PALOMAR COLLEGE | INSTRUCTOR: CHANCE COALTER

What was your inspiration for this piece?

My inspiration was an hourglass shape. To keep it interesting, I wanted a contrasting shape that would complement the legs.

What were your project goals?
Did you use any unique construction methods?

My goal was to challenge myself with new techniques. The legs are bending ply on the inside and edged with cross-grain, shop-sawn veneer applied with hide glue. The faces are shop-sawn veneer using plastic resin.

What challenges did you encounter?

The first challenge was making the two shapes intersect flawlessly. I made the center section as one unit and then cut it into pieces attached separately with joinery. The second challenge was spraying the finish evenly, especially into all the little areas. To do this, I taped off the joints and sprayed everything before assembly.

Did you use any special equipment or software?

SketchUp was used for design, vacuum bags and resawing machines for the veneer, bending jigs with layout lines, and jigs for trimming.

What considerations were given to the product's production efficiency?

It's designed with bending ply and veneer for efficiency and price. The conversion varnish dries instantly, is easy to use, and quickly produces a showroom finish without touch-ups. The edge banding can be cut to fit from a single sheet of veneer on a CNC machine. There's also an option for an acrylic top, which lightens the load for shipping.

DIMENSIONS: 35″ H x 46″ W x 14″ D
WEIGHT: 45 lb.
MATERIALS: Bending ply, glass; lychee, curly maple (veneers)
FINISH: Conversion varnish

HIGH SCHOOL

POST-SECONDARY

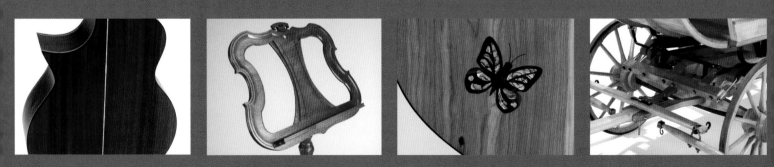

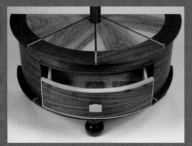
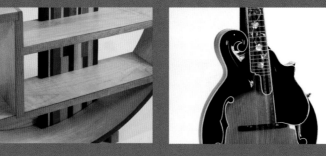

⃝⃝⃝
OPEN

Anything goes in this category! There are no restrictions on style, minimum size, materials, or percent of wood used. Pieces should have originality and functionality. This is the correct place for any projects that don't easily fit other categories, such as musical instruments, lighting, and clocks.

SUNDOWN

KATIE FARNSWORTH

CORNER CANYON HIGH SCHOOL | INSTRUCTOR: TIMOTHY McNEILL

2021
1ST
PLACE

What was your inspiration for this piece?

Some of my earliest memories are of driving for hours in the middle of the desert with classic rock music on the radio. My dad was raised in rural Arizona and we would often visit and go hiking. These great times with music, loved ones, and the outdoors inspired me to create a desert-themed guitar.

What were your project goals?

In addition to creating a playable and well-constructed guitar, my goal for this project was to create a piece of art that would be recognized as Utah's Delicate Arch.

What challenges did you encounter?

Designing and constructing the large arch inlay by hand was very challenging. I chose the grain direction for each piece of veneer to not only be aesthetically appealing, but also to reduce the risk of chipping or breaking while cutting. Because the inlay was so large, small warps in the veneer could later result in gaps or overlapping pieces when gluing into the soundboard. To address this, I flattened the veneer with an iron and excavated an extra 1/4″ at the base of the inlay to give the space needed for the inlay to smooth out and lay flat when it was finally glued down.

Did you use any special equipment or software?

I used several special-made jigs to construct my guitar. One was a form to bend the sides on. The other was a go-bar press to glue struts onto the soundboard and back and to glue the soundboard and back onto the sides of the guitar.

DIMENSIONS: 42″ H x 15.5″ W x 4.5″ D

WEIGHT: 5 lb.

MATERIALS: Spruce, cherry, rosewood, mahogany, maple, various veneers, mother of pearl

FINISH: Boiled linseed oil, lacquer

SERENITY
KEATON CARTER

CORNER CANYON HIGH SCHOOL | INSTRUCTOR: TIMOTHY McNEILL

What was your inspiration for this piece?

When I think of music, I think of peace, joy, and serenity. I wanted to incorporate those feelings. Growing up in Utah, I have developed a deep connection with mountains. The shape of the Tetons is so unique that I knew it would fit perfectly with what I wanted to do.

What were your project goals?

I really wanted to do something that was challenging, different, and awe inspiring. Having created a guitar previously, I had a feel for what was possible and attainable with my skill level. I set out to push that line a little bit further. I also wanted to do everything by hand.

What challenges did you encounter?

My design gave the scene depth, meaning it had background and foreground. How to translate that same effect to veneer? I solved this challenge with double-bevel marquetry. This allowed me to piece the sketch face together with overlapping cutouts that fit nearly seamlessly. I had very little experience with the technique, however, and there was a large learning curve. I designed the scene into sectioned portions that looked like hills, which allowed less re-work when mistakes were made.

Did you use any special equipment or software?

I used a scroll saw to cut the veneer for the sketch face. There was a larger learning curve than I expected. I used a 1/8" piece of melamine particleboard to create a no-clearance base to prevent the veneer from slipping through. I had to use a special dished jig and a vacuum bag in order to glue the face to the soundboard.

DIMENSIONS: 42" H x 16" W x 5" D
WEIGHT: 5 lb.
MATERIALS: Walnut, maple, spruce, various veneers (rosewood, cherry, birdseye maple, etc.)
FINISH: Linseed oil, lacquer

JUNEY BABE
SHANE MOON
CORNER CANYON HIGH SCHOOL | INSTRUCTOR: TIMOTHY McNEILL

2017
1ST
PLACE

What was your inspiration for this piece?
My inspiration came from basic geometry. I wanted to make an original design, something that I had never seen before; something I could call my own that was very clean, but very elegant at the same time.

What were your project goals?
Did you use any unique construction methods?
One of my goals was to make the subtle colors of the Indian rosewood and mother of pearl come to life. I wanted the design to be simple but elegant. I decided to take advantage of contrast, using very dark colors contrasted against very light colors. I didn't want any bright distractions, but rather for the design to flow and work together so that no part was overwhelming. By using only a few basic colors, I was able to bring the subtle beauty out of the materials I was using.

What challenges did you encounter?
My biggest challenge was to place the mother of pearl as edges on the binding; I had seen it done on a guitar before, but I had no clue how to accomplish it. I found no help online or in any guitar-making books. My teacher and I came up with a method using the router, but it was very precise. After everything was said and done, it all worked out perfect and I was happy with my results.

Did you use any special equipment or software?
I used a guitar form to bend the body of the guitar. This was my first time bending wood in such a harsh way. It was very foreign to me. It all worked out okay, despite a few challenges due to the wood cracking on the small part of the bend.

DIMENSIONS: 42″ H x 16″ W x 5″ D
WEIGHT: 5 lb.
MATERIALS: Indian rosewood, ebony, spruce, mother of pearl
FINISH: Lacquer, linseed oil

BLUE GRACE
SAVANNAH RICHARDS

CORNER CANYON HIGH SCHOOL | INSTRUCTOR: TIMOTHY McNEILL

What was your inspiration for this piece?

Ever since my freshman year when I learned about the guitar class, I've wanted to build a guitar. The summer before my senior year started, my family took a trip. While kayaking, I found an abalone shell. So, when I was thinking of potential inlay materials for my guitar, abalone was my first choice. Butterflies have been my favorite animal for as long as I remember, and my favorite color has always been blue, so it all tied together.

What were your project goals?
Did you use any unique construction methods?

My goal at the beginning of the year was to create an art piece good enough that it would be added to the gallery in the hall outside the shop. I'm very pleased that I managed to achieve that. I also learned advanced inlay techniques that I hadn't used on previous projects.

What challenges did you encounter?

Inlay work is very finicky and required me to make allowances for changes as I went. I also accidentally drilled a hole all the way through my soundboard where the inlay was glued in, super-gluing my finished soundboard to the work surface. Unsticking it required carefully shaving off the work surface with long blades.

Did you use any special equipment or software?

To create a symmetrical pattern for the butterflies, I hand-drew the design, scanned it into Photoshop, cut it in half, and mirrored it. To cut the abalone pieces, I had to create a zero-clearance jig. Setting up the fretboard, from pushing in the frets to sanding them to a polish, required a lot of special equipment.

DIMENSIONS: 42″ H x 15.25″ W x 4.5″ D
WEIGHT: 5 lb.
MATERIALS: Cherry, spruce, rosewood (solid, veneer), blue abalone, Abalam
FINISH: Lacquer, linseed oil

2019
2ND
PLACE

ROSETTA
BRAXTON ZARBOCK

CORNER CANYON HIGH SCHOOL | INSTRUCTOR: TIMOTHY McNEILL

What was your inspiration for this piece?

My overall inspiration for this project
was my love for music.

What were your project goals?
Did you use any unique construction methods?

Before I started my project, my goals were to be able
to make something that was unique and individual
to me, and to have something that I could use,
enjoy, and be proud of for my whole entire life. After
completion of my project, I have added some new
goals. First, I want to inspire others to be creative in
the projects that they make; second, I want to do well
in the competitions that I enter my project into.

What challenges did you encounter?

One problem was when I put my wood in the go-
bar press to glue the soundboard to the sides; the
soundboard shifted, and so did the center of the
guitar. To fix this, I had to enlarge the holes drilled
where the neck goes, so I could move the center
of the guitar over to make it look more normal.

Did you use any special equipment or software?

I used a Dremel to cut the inlay on the back and to cut
the rosette. I used the CNC machine to perfectly cut out
the slots for the bridge nut and pins. I used the go-bar
press to glue the struts to the back and soundboard,
and later glue the back and soundboard to the sides. I
used the kerfing jig on the bandsaw to correctly space
out the distance between the cuts on the kerfing.

DIMENSIONS: 40″ H x 14″ W x 4″ D
WEIGHT: 4 lb.
MATERIALS: Rosewood,
mahogany, maple
FINISH: Lacquer, linseed oil

EVERWOOD
SADIE CHIDESTER
CORNER CANYON HIGH SCHOOL | INSTRUCTOR: TIMOTHY McNEILL

2017
2ND
PLACE

What was your inspiration for this piece?

Driving through the Blue Mountains of Oregon is one of my most beautiful and vivid memories. The trees I saw inspired the simple design of the guitar, accentuated with woodburned trees for a more natural appearance, and a complementary organic flow.

What were your project goals?
Did you use any unique construction methods?

I looked at hundreds of guitars to identify small features to create exactly what I wanted. The only thing that I didn't plan out beforehand was the trees. When it came to them, I free-handed everything. My only goal was to make them realistic; not perfect or carefully planned.

What challenges did you encounter?

The biggest challenge was the inlay; I accidentally did the process backward, so creating a seamlessly fitting piece of veneer took several emotionally painful tries and failures. Also, when testing a few ways of doing the trees on the back, a Sharpie technique took a wrong turn. I tried desperately to remove it, but the ink had seeped through the entire piece. It became a faded, shadowy look that I chose to keep.

Did you use any special equipment or software?

I used a woodburning tool, which I was fairly comfortable with. This is my second guitar so, fortunately, most of the process was familiar.

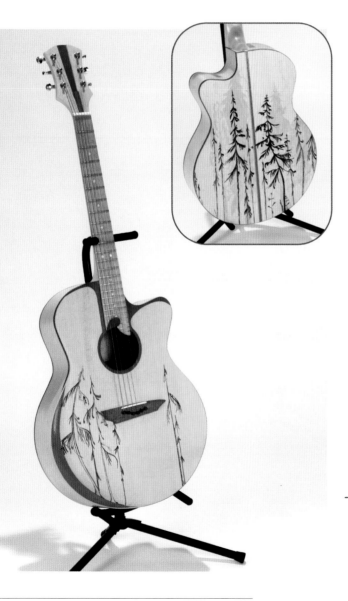

DIMENSIONS: 40″ H x 22″ W x 5″ D

WEIGHT: 5 lb.

MATERIALS: Oak, spruce, maple, African mahogany

FINISH: Linseed oil

ANGRY FISH
MAXWELL STANGE
CADILLAC HIGH SCHOOL | INSTRUCTOR: JASON STANGE

What was your inspiration for this piece?

My main inspiration for this piece is to carry on the art of my grandfather and other local carvers. My grandpa was the one who taught me to carve. I originally started carving fish decoys for ice fishing. However, for this project I wanted to challenge myself by making a complex and realistic fish design. Unlike decoys, this fish was never designed to be used and it serves more as a decorative piece.

What were your project goals?

My goal in creating this project was to make an angry yet realistic looking fish.

What challenges did you encounter?

The most challenging part was creating the posture of the fish. There were many ridges and low spots to carve to achieve an "angry" look. The face also had many fine details to hand-carve. Creating a low spot to insert the eyes proved to be rather difficult and time consuming. Also, the mouth seemed bare without teeth. I finally decided to use rose thorns, which is perhaps the most creative aspect of the project.

Did you use any special equipment or software?

With decoy carving being such a traditional process, the need for CAD and other design software is minimal. The fish is 100% hand carved. I only used knives, chisels, and gouges to shape the wood.

DIMENSIONS: 6″ H x 4″ W x 14″ D
WEIGHT: 4 lb.
MATERIALS: White pine
FINISH: Primer, acrylic paints, spar urethane

QUARTER-SCALE MUD WAGON

ROEHBEN SARKISIAN

NEWBERG SENIOR HIGH SCHOOL | INSTRUCTOR: ROB LEWIS

2017

HM

HONORABLE MENTION

What was your inspiration for this piece?

My inspiration for this piece came from a stagecoach that is roughly 140 years old and has been used every year since it was made. It was first used for mail runs, then stagecoach races, and now it is in the local parade every year. The history behind this specific stagecoach is extremely fascinating, so I wanted to make an authentic replica.

What were your project goals?
Did you use any unique construction methods?

I decided to make this project using the same techniques and in the same order as stagecoach builders would have in the 1850s. I wanted to make it as authentic as possible.

What challenges did you encounter?

This project has been extremely challenging in a lot of ways; it is my third attempt. I originally had to scale down measurements that someone else took, which I found weren't all accurate and some were missing. I got to see the original in person to take measurements myself and see just how everything went together. I drew up a much better set of plans and improved greatly from my first two attempts. This model is as accurate as can be.

Did you use any special equipment or software?

In order to replicate the processes done back in the 1850s, I had to use or create small-scale tools and jigs, such as to cut 1/8″ mortises and tenons, or a 4″ mini table saw with a sideways sled to cut the necks on the spokes. I made a miniature jointer using a spiral bit in a router so I could square up small pieces without losing a finger. I also made a steam bender from PVC pipe and a pressure cooker, as well as a lot of bending jigs.

DIMENSIONS: 24″ H x 20″ W x 72″ D
WEIGHT: 50 lb.
MATERIALS: Cedar, ash, poplar, hickory, elm, leather
FINISH: Shellac

TREBLE

TYLER KEENEY

ROLLA TECHNICAL INSTITUTE | INSTRUCTOR: ROBERT STUDDARD

What was your inspiration for this piece?

My dad got me into music at a young age; through that I have had many great experiences. This piece was made for him and his prized guitar as a thank you for showing me something I would have otherwise overlooked.

What challenges did you encounter? Did you use any unique construction methods?

The treble clef was the most difficult challenge. After steaming the boards for approximately 10 hours and once in a while taking them out and bending and stretching the strips, we would only have a 10-minute window to get the strips bent and glued together before they would start drying out and stiffening. After many tries, I solved this by sanding down the strips to 1/8" and removing them from the steaming box many times to be stretched.

Did you use any special equipment or software?

I used a Homag CNC router to cut the pieces for the rounded top and bottom pieces. I also used a lathe to turn the legs on the bottom. These were both new to me and fun and interesting to learn about.

DIMENSIONS: 42" H x 24" W x 12" D

WEIGHT: 80 lb.

MATERIALS: Hickory, walnut, KerfKore bending plywood

ABULAFIA LECTERN
DOTAN APPELBAUM

CENTER FOR FURNITURE CRAFTSMANSHIP | INSTRUCTOR: TIM ROUSSEAU

2021
1ST
PLACE

What was your inspiration for this piece?

As a maker of Jewish-Moroccan origin, I am particularly inspired by the styles and histories of medieval Iberia-Mudejar style, which refers to art and architecture produced under Christian rule in kingdoms recently reconquered from Islamic Iberia. While the visual styles within Mudejar vary widely, the category is unified by the overwhelming question of how religions share culture within shared societies. This piece was particularly influenced by the Samuel Halevi Abulafia Synagogue in Toledo, Spain. Visually, the design is meant to create balance between a rich fullness of intricate detail, with a striking emptiness. The piece is filled with thoughtful patterns and inscriptions.

What were your project goals?
Did you use any unique construction methods?

This project was made during a course segment on curves; the goal was to try various methods of creating curved forms in wood.

What challenges did you encounter?

The lattice is made of bent laminations of commercial maple veneer in the shape of a sine curve. I tried a variety of techniques and glues to form the curves I needed with a bond that would hold the shape well. The carvings on the aprons required several full weeks of work with Fusion 360 and the CNC. Additionally, the walnut used in this project (all from one slab) presented an additional challenge. The slab appealed to me because of what it offered in color, including sapwood. Knowing that sapwood is generally undesirable in furniture, I had to find ways to include it without making it seem accidental.

Did you use any special equipment or software?

I used Fusion 360, a CNC, and a bending form for the lattice that I cut on the CNC.

DIMENSIONS: 48" H x 20" W x 20" D
WEIGHT: 40 lb.
MATERIALS: Walnut, maple (solid, veneer), Baltic birch plywood
FINISH: Osmo, Mahoney's

MAHOGANY MUSIC STAND

ZALA OUYANG

NORTH BENNET STREET SCHOOL | INSTRUCTOR: DAN FAIA

2019
1ST
PLACE

What was your inspiration for this piece?

My inspiration for this piece is the shape of a violin. The scroll and volute are on the legs; the music stand desk consists of the c-bout, purflings, and bridge of a violin; and I also made the pegs in brass.

What were your project goals?
Did you use any unique construction methods?

This project was intended to teach me the construction of tripod dovetailed legs, using a shaper and making jigs for shaper cutting, long hole boring in the column, long rod turning, carving, and brass hardware turning on a regular wood lathe.

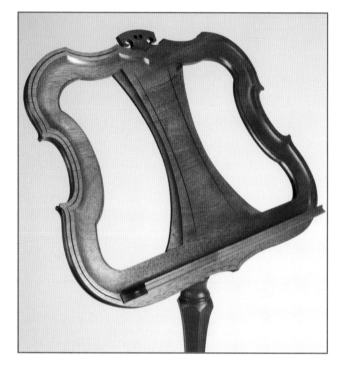

What challenges did you encounter?

I encountered quite a challenge while designing the carving outlines on the legs. I made an extra leg to practice carving on and drawing carving outlines. Also, I could not figure out at first how to make the pegs in brass.

Did you use any special equipment or software?

I made a profile jig for the column to be cut on the shaper. I also carved for the first time on this project.

DIMENSIONS: 50″ H x 20″ W x 17″ D
WEIGHT: 12 lb.
MATERIALS: Mahogany
FINISH: Garnet shellac, aniline dye, Epifanes Varnish, brown wax

GIBSON F-5 MANDOLIN

ED McCRAVY

PALOMAR COMMUNITY COLLEGE | INSTRUCTOR: JACK STONE

2017
1ST
PLACE

What was your inspiration for this piece?

The instrument is modeled after the famous Gibson f-5 Model Mandolin, but in general shape only. My personal innovations make it my own creation. The beauty of any mandolin is seen in its flowing scrolls, delicate horns, and inlay work usually found on the neck and head stock.

What were your project goals?

My personal goal was to make an instrument that would be unique, standing alone in beauty and tone.

What challenges did you encounter?

The cutting and shaping of the scrolls were difficult procedures, involving cutting the front, the inside (block), and the back in the shape of a scroll, with all three pieces having to match perfectly. This involved the use of a bandsaw, scroll saw, and carving knives, as well as rasps and files. The design for the head was first traced with a laser, and then engraved and inlaid by hand. The fretboard, made of solid ebony, was traced from the pattern, excavated, and inlaid entirely by hand. I perfected my own technique for producing the burst of amber coming through the darker edges on the front and back of the instrument, and for the use and spraying of the polyurethane finish.

Did you use any special equipment or software?

Three jigs were constructed to assist in the assembly and alignment of the instrument. These were various commonplace lutherie tools, adapted to fit the construction of a mandolin. A jig for the attachment of the neck to the body was indispensable.

DIMENSIONS: 14″ H x 22″ W x 1.5″ D

WEIGHT: 10 lb.

MATERIALS: Douglas fir, green abalone, ebony, cream plastic binding, tortoise-shell plastic

FINISH: Shellac, amber and darker dyes, clear polyurethane

REVOLUTION MIRROR

SUSAN KOLOSKI

SUNY BUFFALO STATE COLLEGE | INSTRUCTOR: SUNHWA KIM

2021
2ND
PLACE

What was your inspiration for this piece?

This piece is a modern homage to ancient Japanese woodworking. The asymmetrical, horizontal placement of its shelves mimic Japanese watercolor paintings of the setting sun. The title of the piece was conceived from that reference, tying together its circular wood-bent building technique and its symbolic meaning.

What were your project goals?
Did you use any unique construction methods?

The goal for this project was to learn steam-bending. Using MDF, I constructed a jig to the size and form I needed and used six layers of bending plywood with glue between each layer. The jig, with bending plywood on top, was steam-bent overnight.

What challenges did you encounter?

Due to the COVID shutdown, the adhesive-backed wood veneer I bought sat unused over the summer. The backing dried and the plywood warped. This made it unusable for the veneering process and new pieces had to be acquired.

Did you use any special equipment or software?

The bending equipment and machinery were important parts of the construction process.

DIMENSIONS: 60″ H x 45″ W x 20″ D

WEIGHT: 300 lb.

MATERIALS: Walnut, ash

FINISH: Pre-catalyzed lacquer

COUPE DE VILLE MID-CENTURY MODERN BED

ZACHARY SPAHR

PITTSBURG STATE UNIVERSITY | INSTRUCTOR: CHARLIE PHILLIPS

2019 2ND PLACE

What was your inspiration for this piece?

I knew that I wanted to build a bed, and the image that came to mind was an early model Cadillac. I wanted to focus on the luxury of the vehicle while maintaining a low profile. The tufted panels, rosewood veneer panels, and grille were all elements that screamed luxury.

What were your project goals?

There were a few aspects of functionality that I wanted to achieve. The first was to keep it easy to both change the sheets and make the bed. I also wanted to make the bed easy to take apart and low weight so a single person could move and assemble it.

What challenges did you encounter?

I sketched over a hundred profiles and all of them seemed to be missing the spark. I consulted a mentor who advised that I "thin my lines." It took quite a bit of consideration to decipher what he meant, but I finally realized that my leg/foot design seemed too bulky. Also, pulling the four panels together with brass rods turned out to be more challenging than expected. I wanted something that would add rigidity, without an unsightly line across the reveals.

Did you use any special equipment or software?

The AMMT program at Pittsburg State University has access to a wide variety of software and industrial equipment. Software of notable mention would be AutoCAD and Fusion 360 for design, and MasterCAM for programming toolpaths. The tufted panel surfacing was done on an Onsrud 3-axis router. Doweling and a few other toolpaths were programmed on woodWOP and cut on a Weeke BHX 055.

DIMENSIONS: 39" H x 62" W x 84" D

WEIGHT: 85 lb.

MATERIALS: Ribbon sapele, pau ferro veneer, brass

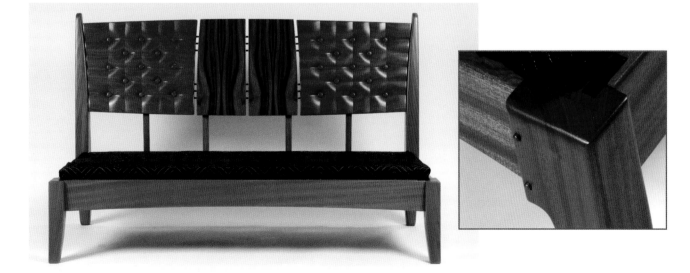

WAVE
CLAIRE SCULLY
CENTER FOR FURNITURE CRAFTSMANSHIP | INSTRUCTOR: ALED LEWIS

What was your inspiration for this piece?
My inspiration shifted throughout the design and making process. What began with an (at the time) accidental squiggle ended with a personal art theory exploration. Although initially designed as a floating entry table, the same form went through various designs that suited other rooms of the home. It is meant to be hung at a height where the first instinct is to slide your hand down the valleys and up the hills, bringing a sense of play.

What were your project goals?
Did you use any unique construction methods?
The brief for this project asked students "to explore the processes required to produce curved components efficiently and accurately." It is the word "explore" that lingered with me through this project. I wanted to discover the different interpretations of a single line, which in turn allowed for flexible functionality in the home. With the brief in mind, I was able to take my drawing, refine it in Fusion 360, and then create the pattern for the four forms required to make the main structure. This meant days spent with the CNC and ten sheets of MDF before the forms could be assembled with PVC pipe and threaded rod. I chose an epoxy with a long curing time, so I was able to stack 28 layers of commercial veneer and clamp it between the single bottom and three top forms.

What challenges did you encounter?
When I failed to find hardware small enough to accommodate a structure that is barely ½" thick, I had to design a bracketing system that would not distract from the line itself, while also ensuring stability.

Did you use any special equipment or software?
I used Autodesk Fusion 360 and the school's ShopBot CNC.

DIMENSIONS: 11" H x 42.3125" W x 8.75" D
WEIGHT: 8 lb.
MATERIALS: European beech (veneer), poplar
FINISH: Old-Fashioned Milk Paint, Sher-Wood KemVar (M, Dull Rubbed Effect)

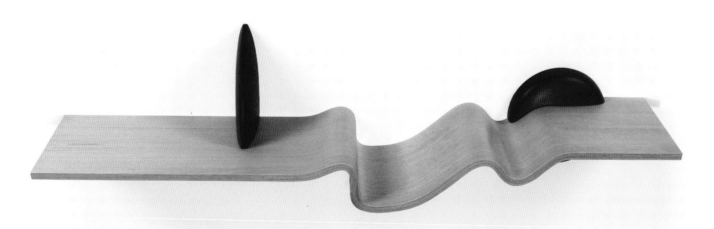

HIBISCUS FLOWERS IN BLOOM

DEREK McDONALD

THE FURNITURE INSTITUTE OF MASSACHUSETTS | INSTRUCTOR: PHILLIP C. LOWE

2017 HM
HONORABLE MENTION

What was your inspiration for this piece?

This piece was inspired by the high-relief work of Grinling Gibbons, a 17th-century English carver famous for his intricate and lifelike cascades of flowers, fruits, and animals. I was immediately taken aback by the beauty and skill of his work and decided to try a project in his style. I chose my wife's favorite flower, the hibiscus, as the subject.

DIMENSIONS: 24" H x 16" W x 5" D
WEIGHT: 10 lb.
MATERIALS: Basswood, cherry, mirror
FINISH: Shellac

What were your project goals?

First and foremost, the goal of this project was to create something beautiful for my wife. Second to that, I wanted to advance my carving skills and decided that using a trial-by-fire approach was the way to achieve that. Prior to this, I had only been carving for a few months in my spare time and wanted to devote a good chunk of time to see what I could learn.

What challenges did you encounter?

When I first saw Gibbons' work, I assumed each was carved from a single solid piece of wood; I learned they are actually built up in layers. My carving has the background layer of the main stem and flowers on each end; the four large blossoms were carved separately. A big challenge was the planning required to carve the large blossoms so they would meet the stem at the correct position and angle, without interfering with the other blossoms. I solved this by making cardboard templates on angled dowels. I then slid the templates on the dowels to get the depths and overlaps figured out, and used the angles of the dowels to cut the stem attachment points.

DIAMOND LAMP

SARAH SLIGHTOM

HERRON SCHOOL OF ART AND DESIGN | INSTRUCTOR: KATIE HUDNALL

2019

F

FINALIST

What was your inspiration for this piece?
I choose a shape each semester that I use for every project I make. In this case, the shape was a diamond. By experimenting with manipulating diamonds, I was able to create a form that I was satisfied with for the project requirements to make a lighting piece.

What were your project goals?
Did you use any unique construction methods?
The goal with this project was to learn how to weld. This is a process and building technique that

I had been interested in learning for a long time. I successfully made many prototypes and a final product with the new knowledge of how to weld.

What challenges did you encounter?
One of my early prototypes lacked an internal structure to hold the frame up. As I was welding it began to collapse and curl in on itself. After that failed prototype, I realized that an internal structure was crucial for the piece to hold its shape and stand on its own.

DIMENSIONS: 24″ H x 11″ W x 11″ D
WEIGHT: 9 lb.
MATERIALS: Cherry (veneer), plywood, metal
FINISH: Shellac

DIAD

HAORAN XUE

AUBURN UNIVERSITY | INSTRUCTOR: TIN-MAN LAU

What was your inspiration for this piece?

I was inspired by multi-function furniture.

What were your project goals?

My goal was to make a creative piece of furniture that would save space. People get the function of two pieces of furniture in one. It's a coffee table, but when there are lots of people and chairs are needed, then it can be easily changed to a chair. It's high quality, stable, and pretty.

What challenges did you encounter?

It was a struggle to adjust the curvature and dimension of each piece to satisfy ergonomics and aesthetics. I also had a small struggle in putting all the wood pieces and glass together.

Did you use any special equipment or software?

I used SolidWorks to build a 3D model to see the proportions and overall look, then fed the design into a CNC router.

DIMENSIONS: 20" H x 42.5" W x 21.75" D
WEIGHT: 72 lb.
MATERIALS: Mahogany MDF, glass
FINISH: Clear satin finish

HIGH SCHOOL

 ### FIRST PLACE

SECOND PLACE

HONORABLE MENTION

FINALIST

POST-SECONDARY

FIRST PLACE

SECOND PLACE

HONORABLE MENTION

FINALIST

SEATING

The seating category includes chairs and other seating pieces such as ottomans, benches, rocking chairs, stools, and settees. Projects may be upholstered. All pieces must actually function as seating; the judges sit on each chair to test the strength of the joints. Comfort, stability, and aesthetics are the primary factors assessed.

THE NEST

MOHAMMED AL-YASEEN

LINCOLN EAST HIGH SCHOOL | INSTRUCTOR: JON HEITHOLD

2021
1ST
PLACE

What was your inspiration for this piece?

This chair piece is inspired by the designs of Robert van Embricqs. The intent of the design was to make something similar to his work with hinging slats. Working primarily from images, I was able to extrapolate some dimensions and put together a CAD model that could lead me forward. The elliptical arrangement of the alternating hinge pattern drew me to this piece. The design lays flat on the floor or hangs flat on the wall and then, with a simple push from the back, the 74 hinged pieces move forward or upward as it may be. Once positioned on the floor, the form is a wonderful lounge chair with deceptive strength and comfort.

What were your project goals?

The overall goal was to achieve a form of symmetry and emphasis and to create a conversation piece. Ultimately, the chair needs to be functional while yet striking enough to stir conversation and inquisition from the viewer.

What challenges did you encounter?

Most challenges dealt with hinge type, jig constructions to aid in drilling holes at the drill press, and maximizing the use of the RWL (random width and length) cherry planks. Prototyping was the best problem solver. Trying different hardware on scrap material and doing some weight tests helped solve some issues.

Did you use any special equipment or software?

I relied on full scale, annotated prints from a wide format plotter to assist with a mock-up model and then dimensions were transferred from the CAD work to S4S (surfaced four sides) cherry hardwood. Drill press jigs to achieve accurate and repeatable drilling operations were most important and made from scratch.

DIMENSIONS: 32″ H x 37″ W x 45″ D
WEIGHT: 34 lb.
MATERIALS: Cherry
FINISH: Tung oil

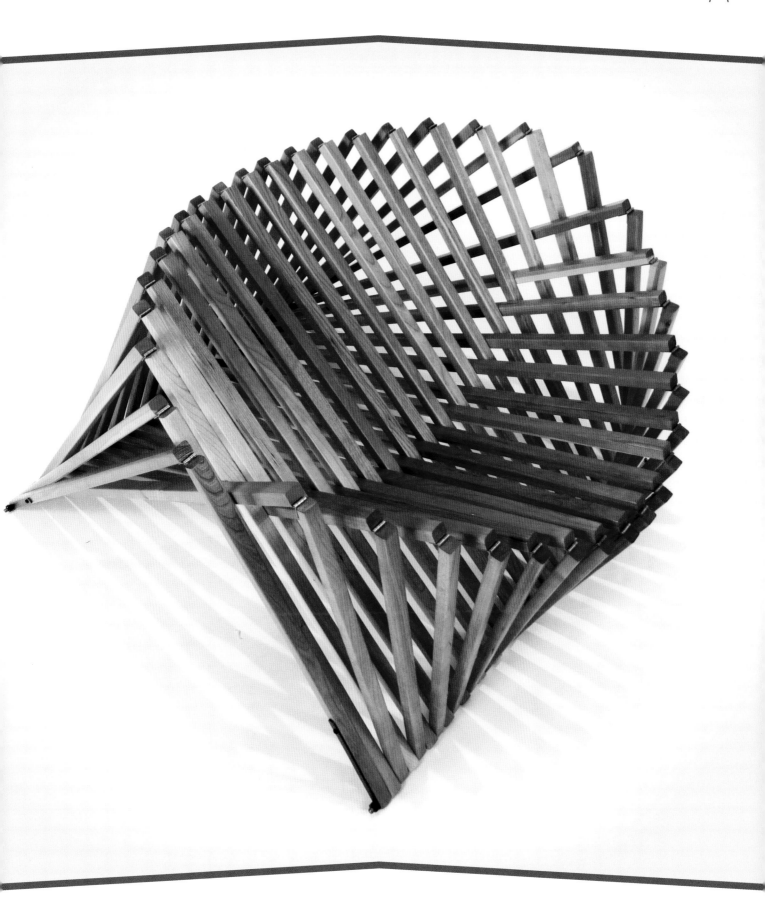

L. & J.G. STICKLEY PRAIRIE CHAIR

LOGAN MILLER

LINCOLN EAST HIGH SCHOOL | INSTRUCTOR: JEFFREY McCABE

2019
1ST
PLACE

What was your inspiration for this piece?

My inspiration for this project was the original L. & J.G. Stickley Prairie Chair. I wanted to make an authentic reproduction; I did not change any details and kept it accurate to the Stickley design.

What challenges did you encounter?

One challenge I had was having to very carefully plan and think about the order in which I glued and finished everything. For example, I had to glue up the frame of the chair before I would be able to glue the corbels on because it would have lost clamping power if I glued up the frame with them on due to the curvature of the corbels.

Did you use any special equipment or software?

In order to veneer the faces of all the upper and lower aprons/rails of the chair, I had to glue it down in our shop vacuum bag using Masonite cauls to keep the veneer in place. I have done a lot of veneering before, but something that was completely new to me was using a hollow chisel mortiser for the mortises.

Was any part of the project created by another person?

I had to order the cushions custom made from a local upholstery shop.

DIMENSIONS: 25.75" H x 39.5" W x 35" D

WEIGHT: 40 lb.

MATERIALS: Quartersawn oak, plainsawn oak, quartersawn white oak (veneer)

FINISH: Golden oak stain, medium walnut stain, tung oil varnish

CONCEPTS IN PARALLEL

SPENCER JOHNSON

CORNER CANYON HIGH SCHOOL | INSTRUCTOR: TIMOTHY McNEILL

2017
1ST
PLACE

What was your inspiration for this piece?
Various elements of design were integrated from a diverse selection of chairs, including the parallel relationship between the seat and armrest of Moser's Lolling Chair and Maloof's Lounge Rocker with its upholstery embedded into the frame.

What were your project goals? Did you use any unique construction methods?
My overall goal throughout the construction of this project was to create something unique that people could sit in, enjoy, and admire. I intended for the entirety of the process to enhance my ability to turn ideas and visions into reality and refine accuracy and precision in craftsmanship.

What challenges did you encounter?
Achieving synergy between stability, strength, aesthetic, and comfort was challenging. Many sketches were made and the rendering in SolidWorks was manipulated many times. The mock-up allowed me to test all four of these important characteristics.

Did you use any special equipment or software?
A 3D rendering of the chair was completed using SolidWorks software. Prior to construction of the final product, I completed a mock-up of the chair. The backrests of the mock-up were used as a jig in the construction of the upholstery. The leather panels of the cushion assemblies were sewn using an industrial sewing machine, which I was taught to use by my friend during the process.

Was any part of the project created by another person?
The upholstery of the chair was modeled in SolidWorks by my friend under my direction.

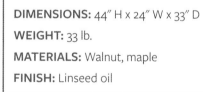

DIMENSIONS: 44″ H x 24″ W x 33″ D
WEIGHT: 33 lb.
MATERIALS: Walnut, maple
FINISH: Linseed oil

ADIRONDACK CHAIR

DAVID OLSON

SAINT CROIX CENTRAL HIGH SCHOOL | INSTRUCTOR: GARRET WENZEL

2021

2ND

PLACE

What was your inspiration for this piece?

The piece is a reproduction of an Adirondack chair. I made the chair with intentional changes to the overall design.

What were your project goals?

My project goals were to make a clean-looking wood project without the use of screws or nails. The chair is solely held together with wooden biscuits, dowels, and glue.

What challenges did you encounter?

Some of the challenges for this project were joining the boards with only dowels and biscuits. This was challenging because I had never done a project of this size with dowels and biscuits. Another challenge was getting the angle and alignment of the legs correct.

Did you use any special equipment or software?

I used a CAD program to help with the design of the legs. I also used a CNC router and a biscuit joiner.

DIMENSIONS: 38″ H x 23.5″ W x 41.5″ D

WEIGHT: 30 lb.

MATERIALS: Walnut, maple

FINISH: Shellac

SINKING CHAIR

KATJA PEEREBOOM

CEDAR RIDGE HIGH SCHOOL | INSTRUCTOR: KEITH YOW

What was your inspiration for this piece?

I was inspired by furniture that I saw on Pinterest, especially by furniture that had pieces that sank when pressure was applied to them. The Sitskie Block Armchair was a definite jumping block for the design of my chair that I referenced, especially in the beginning, for inspiration and ideas.

What were your project goals?
Did you use any unique construction methods?

My goal was to create a chair that looked normal but had a surprise element—the sinking aspect of the blocks. I also wanted to create a chair that I could sit in like I do in larger armchairs: sideways, with my legs crossed, with one of my legs through the armrest, or one over the armrest. This chair was something that I wanted to build to work for me.

What challenges did you encounter?

I faced many challenges when constructing this chair. The biggest difficulty was constructing the support system so it was both supportive and comfortable. I solved this by building a prototype that helped me figure out the issues with my original design.

Did you use any special equipment or software?

I used bungee cords and hog rings as a way to secure and attach the blocks to the chair. I also used a Domino machine.

DIMENSIONS: 43″ H x 23″ W x 28″ D
WEIGHT: 52 lb.
MATERIALS: Walnut (solid, veneer), poplar, plywood, cherry
FINISH: Varathane water-based polyurethane

A ROCK IN THE RIGHT DIRECTION

CHRISTOPHER KLEIN

PRINCETON DAY SCHOOL | INSTRUCTOR: CHRIS MAHER

2017
2ND
PLACE

What was your inspiration for this piece?

I was inspired to build this rocking chair because of my dad. My grandfather gave my dad a rocking chair years ago. My dad loves this chair and sits in it every day, whether he is reading, watching television, or putting on his shoes. Unfortunately, it is now falling apart. This gave me the idea of building a new and more modern rocking chair for my dad.

What were your project goals?
Did you use any unique construction methods?

My most important project goal was to make a comfortable, attractive rocking chair that rocked smoothly. I also wanted to take a traditional design and reinterpret it into the contemporary era, hence the title.

What challenges did you encounter?

There were many different design and construction challenges. I never imagined how much math went into building a rocking chair! I had to use trigonometry and pi as I designed my chair, which was a new challenge for me. One of the hardest challenges was making the rockers; they needed to be identical and to fit into the rest of the chair perfectly. Using templates helped a lot. Another challenge was the Danish cord seat.

Did you use any special equipment or software?

I had to use many different jigs.

DIMENSIONS: 33″ H x 24″ W x 30″ D
WEIGHT: 24 lb.
MATERIALS: Cherry
FINISH: Boiled linseed oil, tung oil

THE LIMBERT

CAIDELL DAVIS

LINCOLN EAST HIGH SCHOOL | INSTRUCTOR: JEFFREY McCABE

What was your inspiration for this piece?

Upon sorting through the selection of woods we had in stock at school, I couldn't help but appreciate the beautiful ray-flake quartersawn oak. And, because of my love for Mission-style work, I knew I had to use it to build some reproduction of a Mission-style object. I soon found exactly what I was looking for in a dusty old Arts and Crafts history book on our woodshop bookshelf. My piece is intended to be an authentic reproduction of the original window bench produced by Charles P. Limbert. It is constructed with the same unique angles and mortise-and-tenon joinery that Limbert used in the early 1900s. I enjoy the Mission-style look of the piece, and the fact that it can be used in a variety of ways (a bench, a footstool, a step stool, etc.).

What challenges did you encounter?

The most challenging part of building this piece was to recreate all of the different angles that make the design interesting. Each leg has two different tapers for each edge, and a third angle for the long mortise of the side panel. None of these angles were the same. Some form of angled jig was necessary for everything from cutting the legs and shaping the angled tenons to clamping the finished frame together.

DIMENSIONS: 24″ H x 26″ W x 18″ D
WEIGHT: 28 lb.
MATERIALS: Ray-flake quartersawn oak
FINISH: Two-part stain, tung oil

Did you use any special equipment or software?

When it came to cutting the four square accents from the side panels, I drew a program for our GlenTek Warthog CNC using AutoCAD 2019 and transferred it through EnRoute 6 to produce a .TAP file with two bridges per square to prevent the leftover pieces from coming completely loose. I also designed a second file with the appropriate depth and angle to cut my long mortises that hold the side panel. It took a lot of accuracy in the piece-building process to achieve the symmetry and precision the bench requires.

Was any part of the project created by another person?

The only manufactured element of this piece is the cushion.

ROWAN'S ROCKER

HOPE EDMISTON

CORNER CANYON HIGH SCHOOL | INSTRUCTOR: TIMOTHY McNEILL

What was your inspiration for this piece?

The rocker was made for my 4-year-old brother, Rowan. Two years ago, he was diagnosed with autism. This means he has a hard time communicating, and it's also hard to sit still. I created the rocker as a therapeutic way to counteract these two problems. Someone could sit next to him, and the movement allows him to concentrate enough to have a conversation. My brother uses it every day, and it's built a stronger relationship between us.

What were your project goals?
Did you use any unique construction methods?

The project's goals were to use a complicated bend and mortise-and-tenon joints.

What challenges did you encounter?

The hardest challenge was bending the sides. The sides were too thick to only steam bend, and if I wanted most of the side to be in one piece I wouldn't be able to laminate bend it either. I steamed the sides in 1/4″ slivers, and then I bent the pieces together onto the form. After they dried, I bent them over the form again with glue between the slivers so that I had a solid piece. Another problem was I feared the legs would snap under weight, so I added the bottom curve on the sides and the bottom rail.

Did you use any special equipment or software?

This entire project was a dive into new equipment for me. I'd never before used steam chambers, bending forms, handplanes, chisels, or mortising machines in my experience as a woodworker.

DIMENSIONS: 35.25″ H x 49.125″ W x 40.5″ D

WEIGHT: 40 lb.

MATERIALS: Cherry, ash, mahogany

FINISH: Linseed oil

DOBLE PLACER

ZACH STUDDARD

ROLLA TECHNICAL INSTITUTE | INSTRUCTOR: ROBERT STUDDARD

What was your inspiration for this piece?

My inspiration for this piece was a Sam Maloof rocker I wanted to make for my senior project. I researched several versions that were all similar to Sam's, but I liked Charles Brock's style best. I did not want to completely copy the chair (there was only one Sam), so I made a few changes to fit my style, including making it a double rocker.

What were your project goals?
Did you use any unique construction methods?

My goal for this rocker was to incorporate some new technologies or methods into the construction of the chair. The judges in the 2015 contest said they wanted to see the students branch out and try new things. I decided to tackle the seat with our Weeke CNC router. The programming of the seat was very complex and took about three weeks. I also felt I needed to spotlight some of the new finish technologies.

What challenges did you encounter?

I could not find any plans or dimensions for a double rocker. I eventually took the single rocker plans and doubled the bottom and headrest, then subtracted the distance of one side of the seat off the center. Using only seven spindles as called for in the single rocker plans left a big gap in the center, so I added two more. After trying to figure out the placement mathematically, I decided to go with what was pleasing to the eye.

Did you use any special equipment or software?

I used AutoCAD to design the seat and patterns for the chair and woodWOP on the CNC.

DIMENSIONS: 52″ H x 48″ W x 48″ D

WEIGHT: 100 lb.

MATERIALS: Native Missouri walnut, maple, wenge

FINISH: ML Campbell walnut dye stain, ML Campbell MagnaMax satin lacquer, Johnson clear paste wax

HARP BACK CHAIR

AVROM TOBIN

NORTH BENNET STREET SCHOOL | INSTRUCTOR: DAN FAIA

2021
1ST
PLACE

What was your inspiration for this piece?

This piece is based on a chair at the Metropolitan Museum of Art that is attributed to Duncan Phyfe. I intended to make a chair loosely based on the original, but though research, practice, and development, I created more of a reproduction than originally planned.

What were your project goals?

My goals were to build a chair using a joinery method differing from a more traditional dining chair I had previously made; to include tapered reeds running from the top of the posts to the front of the chair; to reproduce the complex carvings found on the original chair; and to improve the feet.

What challenges did you encounter?

The main challenge was how to make it strong enough with the weaker construction method. This involved using large tenons that had to miss each other and the use of twin tenons on the front and back rail for added strength and stability. The front rail needed a stub tenon to prevent racking, which had to miss the large tenon from the side rail; it also has a long tenon to provide adequate strength.

Did you use any special equipment or software?

I used a tapered reeding box that allowed for reeds to be cut in a line by scratch stock, regardless if the surface was flat or not. I used a planing jig to establish the relationship between the front and back and inside joinery to create the proper tapered shape of the posts using the planer. This was also used on the mortising machine to cut the mortises at the proper angle. Shaping the crest rail and excavating the frame for the veneer almost all had to be done by hand.

DIMENSIONS: 32.5″ H x 18″ W x 21″ D
WEIGHT: 30 lb.
MATERIALS: Mahogany, maple burl (veneer), ash, fabric, horse hair
FINISH: Shellac, SeedLac, Polylac, wax

COOPERED DAYBED

OSAMU SASSA

CENTER FOR FURNITURE CRAFTSMANSHIP | INSTRUCTOR: ALED LEWIS

What was your inspiration for this piece?

The curved profile is designed to gently support a person using it as a bench or reclining surface. The coopered form is cut parallel to the ground plane, revealing an elliptical perimeter. A set of legs splay out at a slight angle and are held inward by a single curved stretcher connected in tension to the underside of the coopered top.

What were your project goals?
Did you use any unique construction methods?

The primary goal was to create a piece that was comfortable. Time was initially spent studying scale and curved radiuses to accommodate the proportions of the human body. To test comfort, the coopered form was milled out of 4″ rigid foam insulation using the CNC. For the ash pieces, a router jig acting as a gantry running on two rails was used to cut the top edges of the coopered shape parallel to the deck plane.

What challenges did you encounter?

Cutting templates and making shaping jigs for the nearly 33′ radius staves was greatly aided by the use of the CNC. Cutting the coopered form using the router jig was also challenging.

Did you use any special equipment or software?

I used the CNC and the software Fusion 360 for the first time to mill 4″ rigid foam to verify comfort of the coopered form and to cut the shaper jigs for the staves. I made a large router jig (roughly 32″ x 96″) to cut the coopered shape parallel to the deck plane.

DIMENSIONS: 15″ H x 83″ W x 26″ D

WEIGHT: 55 lb.

MATERIALS: Ash

FINISH: Spray lacquer, super-blonde shellac

C.S. WONG

MAGGI WONG

THE KRENOV SCHOOL | INSTRUCTOR: LAURA MAYS

What was your inspiration for this piece?

One day in a used bookstore, I discovered a book of photographs from early 20th century Hong Kong. As I flipped through the pages, I stopped at a full-page photo of a fishing boat with a large rectangular sail that tapered at the top, with horizontal bars from top to bottom. The boat was filled with people sitting peacefully, floating in the waters of the Zhujiang River estuary in the South China Sea. This image resonated deeply with me because of the stories I heard of my father and his best friend who, during the Cultural Revolution in China, decided to swim through that same body of water to flee to British-occupied Hong Kong for a better life. I knew I wanted to share his history through this chair.

What were your project goals?
Did you use any unique construction methods?

I wanted to incorporate curved design elements with my inspiration from the sail of the boat, and I wanted to pursue a woodworking approach that would be entirely new to me, namely steam bending, to achieve graceful curves through the application of steam to wood before including it in the frame.

DIMENSIONS: 37″ H x 22″ W x 25″ D

WEIGHT: 40 lb.

MATERIALS: Eucalyptus

FINISH: Platinum-blonde shellac

What challenges did you encounter?

As there are many species and varieties of eucalyptus, the parameters for optimal steam bending were largely guesswork and experimentation. The solution was presoaking rough-milled stock for at least four days in PVC pipes, then placing it into a preheated steam box for about two hours before immediately placing it into the form and winching it into the curve. An additional construction challenge was creating a curved joint where the side rails met the back leg perfectly without taking too much length off the side rail, which could jeopardize the originally intended curve and possibly shorten the armrest.

JOINED ARTS & CRAFTS CHAIR IN WALNUT & LEATHER

DANIEL OSACH

NORTH BENNET STREET SCHOOL | INSTRUCTOR: DAN FAIA

2021

2ND PLACE

What was your inspiration for this piece?

This chair was copied from the Arts and Crafts chair made by our master instructor. His original patterns were used to create the patterns for this chair, with no changes. Every effort was made to copy his craftsmanship in style, technique, and proportion.

What were your project goals?
Did you use any unique construction methods?

Our project goals were to learn to use the unique machine setups required to create and fit the angled joinery needed to build this chair.

What challenges did you encounter?

Getting the splat to rest at the correct angle to meet the crest rail in space was difficult. It was found by shaving the tenons on one face and gluing veneer to the opposite face to compensate in the right direction. Shaped repeating cloud motifs appear on all the rails. A pierced splat is dry fitted as one, and then sawed into three before glue up.

Did you use any special equipment or software?

Table saws, router tables, and a mortising machine were used to create the angled joinery. A simple jig and guide were used to angle the splat in space to meet the crest rail.

DIMENSIONS: 39" H x 24" W x 14" D
WEIGHT: 18 lb.
MATERIALS: Black walnut, pine, sipo, ash, hemp webbing, thin burlap, nylon bridle stitching, curled horsehair stuffing, cotton muslin, cotton batting, leather
FINISH: Boiled linseed oil, super-blonde shellac, conversion varnish

2019
2ND
PLACE

MARITZA'S BENCH

ALEXANDER LOHN

CENTER FOR FURNITURE CRAFTSMANSHIP | INSTRUCTOR: ALED LEWIS

What was your inspiration for this piece?
The inspiration for this piece was two-fold. The first inspiration was to fulfill many learning objectives I had, such as fitted, hand-cut dovetail drawers, frame-and-panel construction, and case construction. The second inspiration was wanting to make a gift for my parents to go into their entryway.

What challenges did you encounter?
There were a variety of elements I did not know how I would accomplish, such as the angle on the side shelves, and the joinery of the legs into the top rail where a cross-rail hits at the same point. In these instances, I went over examples with teachers at the school as well as doing more detailed full-scale drawings. A traditional frame and panel construction did not meet the overall aesthetic for the sliding door. I did many drawings of different ideas but ended up designing

a frame-and-panel construction that had the frame overlapping the side rails of the frame, with the handles being incorporated into the overall construction.

Did you use any special equipment or software?
I built a series of jigs to accomplish the case construction. I also built a jig for cutting the mortises in the miters with a plunge router, as well as a jig for the housed stub tenon mortises. I used a mortiser for much of the joinery for the bench portions.

DIMENSIONS: 17" H x 51.5" W x 14" D
WEIGHT: 58 lb.
MATERIALS: Hard maple, Danish cord
FINISH: Tinted oil

MALOOF-STYLE ROCKER

FARRON KOLB

PALOMAR COLLEGE | INSTRUCTOR: JERRY BEAUDRY

2017
2ND
PLACE

What was your inspiration for this piece?

The first time I saw a Sam Maloof rocker, I fell in love with it and I knew I wanted to make Sam Maloof rockers. When I read that Sam passed away in 2008, I thought that I would never have the opportunity to make one. Having a desire to make furniture, I enrolled in the local woodworking program only to find, much to my joy, that they offered a chair-making class taught by an instructor who actually studied under Sam Maloof for many years. My hope and enthusiasm were rekindled; my goal to learn how to make Sam Maloof rockers could actually become a reality. When making this chair, I tried to emulate Sam Maloof as best I could. Having a mentor who actually knew Sam, worked with Sam, and was able to make copies of Sam's jigs and patterns was more than I could ever have hoped for.

What challenges did you encounter?

I found the construction very challenging, yet extremely rewarding. The joinery of the legs and the way the spindles fit was unique. Once my instructor explained how they fit together, I was able to learn the technique and skills to assemble the chair. I am extremely grateful that I am able to be enrolled in a program that has taught me techniques and skills that I can use in the production of the furniture I plan to make in the future.

DIMENSIONS: 48″ H x 28″ W x 48″ D

WEIGHT: 28 lb.

MATERIALS: Curly shedua, curly maple

FINISH: Liberon oil

2021
HM
HONORABLE
MENTION

QUEEN ANNE CHAIR

JOSEPH THIBEAULT

NORTH BENNET STREET SCHOOL | INSTRUCTOR: DAN FAIA

What was your inspiration for this piece?

I was inspired by traditional Queen Anne chairs. This is an original design of a tenoned chair.

What were your project goals?
Did you use any unique construction methods?

My goals in this piece were to carve veneered volutes in the back splat and to extend the veneer into the crest rail, ultimately creating an inlay as well as a veneered surface.

What challenges did you encounter?

This project was an interesting challenge; I had to cut the top of the veneer to the projection past the crest rail in order to scribe it into the crest rail. I then fixed the veneer to the splat and inlaid it into the crest rail at the same time.

DIMENSIONS: 46″ H x 19″ W x 14″ D
WEIGHT: 25 lb.
MATERIALS: Walnut (solid, crotch veneer)

Was any part of the project created by another person?

The period textiles and upholstery are from Eaton Hill Textiles in Vermont.

STUFFED SAPELE

SAM GALLIART

PITTSBURG STATE UNIVERSITY | INSTRUCTOR: JORDAN BACKS

2019
HM
HONORABLE
MENTION

What was your inspiration for this piece?

I took my inspiration from upholstered fabric chairs and brought it to life out of wood.

What were your project goals?
Did you use any unique construction methods?

The focal point of my chair is definitely the backrest, which is machined entirely out of solid sapele. It catches a lot of people off guard; they do a double-take because they think it is fabric. There is some fairly nontraditional joinery that can be seen on this chair where pieces have been spliced together. This is because I took a pile of scrap wood that was destined for the dumpster and turned it into a piece of furniture.

What challenges did you encounter?

I built a quick prototype out of MDF and wood from a pallet to get the overall proportions. After sitting in the prototype, I realized it wasn't very comfortable. I was able to modify some of the angles of the chair and change the sculpted profile of the seat to make it surprisingly comfortable.

Did you use any special equipment or software?

I used AutoCAD to do most of my modeling for the chair structure. For the upholstered backrest, I used a combination of Fusion 360 and Blender. I also used MasterCAM for all of the CNC programming. The backrest was machined on a four-axis CNC router. The rest of the chair was made by hand with basic woodworking machinery. This chair could have been manufactured solely with the CNC router, but I like to couple automated technology with personal craftsmanship.

DIMENSIONS: 37″ H x 17.5″ W x 24″ D

WEIGHT: 35 lb.

MATERIALS: Sapele

FINISH: Danish oil, paste wax

RECIDIVUS

SCOTT NELSON

THE KRENOV SCHOOL | INSTRUCTOR: LAURA MAYS

What was your inspiration for this piece?

This is a reproduction piece. It is the Danish chair NV45 designed by Finn Juhl. I love the classic form of this iconic Danish chair. There are so many interesting animal-like shapes and forms in this chair.

What were your project goals?
Did you use any unique construction methods?

I wanted to learn to use spokeshaves, rasps, files, carving tools, and coopered planes. This piece is really a functional sculpture. The legs were turned with the protrusion left unshaped. The tenons were all turned using a wrench to check the diameter.

What challenges did you encounter?

The first challenge was locating the joinery in the arm and leg system. The joinery had to load together all as one. There was a lot of mocking up to find the right angles. The shaping was another major challenge. The underside of the arm is such a specific radius I had to make two custom round bottom planes to waste the material away. The underside of the arm also comes to such a thin wing that I was tapping on it and using sounds to determine consistent thickness.

Did you use any special equipment or software?

I made many jigs to repeat my angles for joinery and used drawing extensively to get my head around the unusual shapes of all the parts.

DIMENSIONS: 28″ H x 19″ W x 26″ D
WEIGHT: 31 lb.
MATERIALS: Brazilian mahogany, leather
FINISH: Liberon oil

2019

F

FINALIST

LOW-BACK CHAIR

STEVEN CARTER

PALOMAR COLLEGE | INSTRUCTOR: JERRY BEAUDRY

What was your inspiration for this piece?

My inspiration was the Maloof lowback chair. I did not restrict myself to making an authentic reproduction, but did not intentionally change details.

What were your project goals?
Did you use any unique construction methods?

My goals were to learn the basics of chair design, as well as the joinery featured in Maloof chairs. I also wanted to explore a sculptural approach to woodworking.

What challenges did you encounter?

The biggest challenge was sculpting the arms and crest rail to provide a cohesive feel to the chair. I would spend hours on one side of the chair slowly getting to the look I wanted, and was then able to match the other side in a relatively short time.

Did you use any special equipment or software?

I used matched router bits for the joints. New to me was the use of angle grinders with an Arbortech cutter, as well as a Holey Galahad cutter for roughing out the seat contours. A 6″ random-orbital sander with a contour pad refined the shape. To this point, all of my woodworking was rectilinear, and this process was anything but.

DIMENSIONS: 33″ H x 26″ W x 22″ D

WEIGHT: 10 lb.

MATERIALS: African mahogany, ebony

FINISH: Liberon Finishing Oil, paste wax

2019
F
FINALIST

OBLIO CHAIR

RICHARD MILLER

SEATTLE CENTRAL COLLEGE | INSTRUCTOR: JEFF WASSERMAN

What was your inspiration for this piece?

I have always wanted to design and build a chair, and inspiration came from my desire to bring a fresh take on the Mid-Century Modern furniture that I admire. The oval shape is a design element that I think works well to create an inviting look and adds visual contrast.

What were your project goals?

I wanted to utilize the powerful capabilities of the CNC while developing my own joinery techniques that incorporated more traditional woodworking concepts.

What challenges did you encounter?

To determine the proportions and angles for this chair, I built a crude adjustable prototype. As I wanted the chair to be comfortable for a wide range of people, I sought input from others. There was no consensus on what was appropriate. I ultimately had to pick a direction that felt good and go with it. The construction method was not obvious and there were points where once certain pieces were joined, it became difficult to access and connect other pieces of the chair.

Did you use any special equipment or software?

The 4x10 CNC machine was an integral tool in the production of this chair. I utilized SketchUp as the primary design tool, which needed to be transferred into VCarve for generating tool paths, which was an empowering experience.

DIMENSIONS: 29″ H x 25.5″ W x 27″ D
WEIGHT: 37 lb.
MATERIALS: White maple Europly, birch, Domino tenons, Wilsonart plastic laminate
FINISH: Wipe-on polyurethane

MT. ROCKVALE STOOL

TYLER WILLMON

CENTER FOR FURNITURE CRAFTSMANSHIP | INSTRUCTOR: ALED LEWIS

2019

F

FINALIST

What was your inspiration for this piece?

The stool was made to pair with the Mt. Rockvale Vanity piece (see p. 45), although it is well suited to stand on its own. The vanity mirror "mountain" inspired me to subtly arch the back of the stool.

What were your project goals?
Did you use any unique construction methods?

The goal behind the stool was to incorporate a curvature technique that was part of our curvature course segment. I wanted to explore coopering. When I exhausted sketching, I began to carve away mini Solo cups to find the form I was searching for. Voila! I wanted the joinery to be subtle, so continuing the staves into the legs made perfect sense.

What challenges did you encounter?

As natural as making the staves and legs into one component sounded, deciding where to hide or highlight the details proved troublesome. It was solved by doing an extensive array of mock-ups.

Was any part of the project created by another person?

The upholstery work was done by my brother-in-law Cobi Ferguson of Tate's Upholstery in Rockvale, Tennessee.

DIMENSIONS: 23″ H x 21″ W x 14″ D
WEIGHT: 13 lb.
MATERIALS: White oak, brass, upholstery
FINISH: Osmo Wood Wax Finish (White, Cognac), Osmo Satin Matte Polyx-Oil

THE LOST CALL

ERICA ALBERTSON

UNIVERSITY OF IDAHO | INSTRUCTOR: JAY PENGILLY

What was your inspiration for this piece?

I drew inspiration from what we take for granted in life—time well spent with loved ones and the outdoors, like my favorite memories with my grandmother on her back patio. The curvilinear structural system represents the dynamic forms we find in nature and also reminds me of the curvy woman my grandmother was.

What were your project goals?
Did you use any unique construction methods?

The main goal of this piece was for all elements to be bent wood. The secondary goal was to create an overall comfortable place to sit, which was achieved by the large seat size and tall back to rest the head.

What challenges did you encounter?

Bending wood proved to be a huge challenge, as shorter pieces do not bend as easily as pieces that have more torque. In an attempt to waste as little as possible, I had to steam short pieces in order to bend them. The seat and back had to be bent in a vacuum bag, which required building a second form.

DIMENSIONS: 56" H x 26" W x 30" D
WEIGHT: 50 lb.
MATERIALS: Walnut (solid, veneer), plywood
FINISH: Danish oil

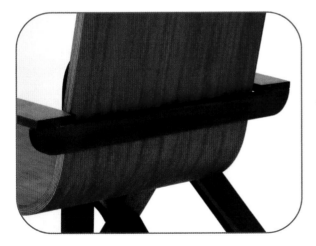

LAVIDA
CHENCHEN FAN
ART CENTER COLLEGE OF DESIGN | INSTRUCTOR: JOHN FORD

What was your inspiration for this piece?
The visual sense of the design was inspired by a thin strip of sky I once saw that moved me and gave me a sense of hope. The impact comes from the contrast between the positive and negative space. I also really like the motion of playing piano; the touch of my finger on the keys greatly inspired this design. Another influence was from a few products—the back curve of a Ming chair, which brings a sense of comfortable embrace, and the transitional surface on a Ferrari F430.

What were your project goals?
Did you use any unique construction methods?
My goal was to translate and combine nature with modern elements to achieve a balance in aesthetics and structure.

What challenges did you encounter?
The most challenging part was using the fiberglass to strengthen the connection between the arms and seat because it is the only connection.

Did you use any special equipment or software?
I used SolidWorks to make a 3D model first. I also made a mold for hot-glue curving the plywood for the top shell. I made a special sanding tool and spent a lot of time on sanding to get smooth surface. The bottom metal support and white oak legs were made by CNC.

DIMENSIONS: 32" H x 26" W x 21" D

WEIGHT: 200 lb.

MATERIALS: Plywood, white oak, fiberglass, metal

FINISH: Matte white and black paint

MODULAR STOOLS

RYAN ZIMMERMAN

EDINBORO UNIVERSITY | INSTRUCTOR: KAREN ERNST

What was your inspiration for this piece?

When I was designing this piece, I had just begun investigating modular furniture. I was intrigued by finding ways to give a functional piece of furniture an alternate layer of function. For the form, I was inspired by Thomas Hucker's Side Chair. I knew I wanted a seat that was visually light, and from its side was a hollow vessel. I was also interested in it being backless. I explored a variety of angles for the seat that would encourage the user to sit upright, negating the need for a back support.

What were your project goals?

The goal was to create a modular system of furniture pieces that could function individually or together. To accomplish this, the design of the stool is the same shape when flipped, giving the piece no defined top or bottom. Also, each plane in the form's construction tapers in and out 1″ from both sides at each joint. This shaping around the perimeter acts as a sort of key that connects the stools into one another.

What challenges did you encounter?

The construction of this series was a bit of a learning curve, since I had never used bent lamination before.

Did you use any special equipment or software?

To achieve the bent portions, I used VacuPress's pump and bag. I started off making a form for my desired curve out of MDF. I then placed six pieces of 1/8″ cherry veneer in the bag over my MDF form to create the radius. When it came to cutting the miters on the bent panels, I created a jig that would cradle the pieces while attached to a crosscut sled.

DIMENSIONS: 18″ H x 18″ W x 21″ D
WEIGHT: 10 lb.
MATERIALS: Cherry (solid, veneer)
FINISH: General Finishes Gel Topcoat, Johnson's paste wax

 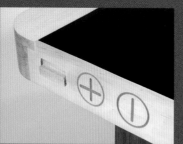  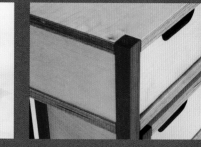

HIGH SCHOOL

🔖 FIRST PLACE

🔖 SECOND PLACE

POST-SECONDARY

🔖 FIRST PLACE

🔖 SECOND PLACE

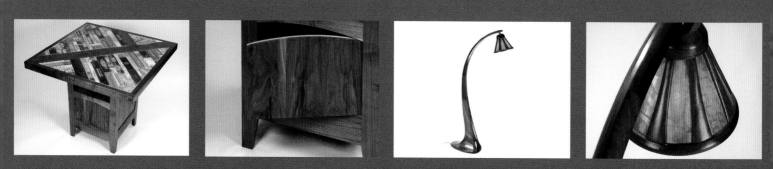

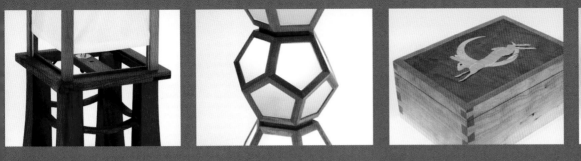

SPECIAL THEME

Each Fresh Wood contest has a special category that is different from the previous one. 2021's special theme was remote woodworking. Students displayed what they built while learning remotely, or a project that was affected by the unusual conditions of that school year. Sports and games were featured in 2019. In 2017, the special theme was lighting.

SHAKER BEDSIDE TABLE

ANDREW TONDU

FRANKFORT HIGH SCHOOL | INSTRUCTOR: DAVID BARRESI

2021
1ST
PLACE

What was your inspiration for this piece?
The inspiration is a simple Shaker-style bedside table with a drawer. I intended to make a reproduction, but modifications were made based on equipment availability and expertise.

What were your project goals?
Did you use any unique construction methods?
The goals were to build a Shaker table virtually using SketchUp and to experience the methods of mass production. Unique design elements included tapered legs—made using a shop-made tapering jig—a beveled top, and mortise-and-tenon joints. The drawer was constructed with a locking rabbet joint with pinned twin tenons attaching the drawer rails to the legs.

What challenges did you encounter?
Due to quarantine, last year's projects were not finished, so we decided to incorporate them into this project. The previously made parts were all different sizes, so they had to be re-sized and re-cut. Time constraints posed a challenge because some of the production took longer than a class period.

Did you use any special equipment or software?
SketchUp Maker 2017 was used to make a scale dimensioned drawing, exploded views, assembly drawing, renderings, and a 60-second animation of the assembly process of the table.

DIMENSIONS: 28″ H x 18″ W x 18″ D
WEIGHT: 17 lb.
MATERIALS: Cherry, walnut, maple, ash, oak, poplar
FINISH: Sprayed lacquer finish

THE BIG SLICK

KYLE HASSETT

DALE JACKSON CAREER CENTER | INSTRUCTOR: JOSEPH DAVIS

What was your inspiration for this piece?

I love to play poker, especially Texas Hold'em, with my dad and brothers. I knew I wanted to build a poker table, but not like one you have seen before. I like Texas Hold'em tables, but thought I could take it a step farther by making it curve around the dealer. Another thing that I really wanted to figure out was how to do a convex arm rest.

What were your project goals?

I wanted to challenge myself on this project, so I tried to incorporate curves into every piece that I could; also, I wanted to do some veneer work whenever I had the chance.

What challenges did you encounter?

The only design problem I ran into was the shape of the top. It was hard to duplicate the shape of the top identically, so I had to use the original EnRoute file to shape and cut out the top and apron.

Did you use any special equipment or software?

The only specialized equipment I used was a CNC.

DIMENSIONS: 34″ H x 80″ W x 36″ D

WEIGHT: 200 lb.

MATERIALS: Sapele (solid, veneer), walnut, birdseye maple (veneer), MDF, KerfKore, Baltic birch plywood, red oak

FINISH: Pre-catalyzed lacquer

DODICI

GIULIA GERSCHEL

PRINCETON DAY SCHOOL | INSTRUCTOR: CHRIS MAHER

What was your inspiration for this piece?

For a long time, I had been looking to replace a worn-out lamp in our dining room; this competition gave me the perfect opportunity. The idea for the dodecahedrons came from the fact that these intricate 12-sided shapes are, to me, an elegant balance of complexity and simplicity.

What were your project goals?

My goal was to create a beautiful, self-standing, light-emitting object.

What challenges did you encounter?

The dodecahedron proved to be much more complicated than I anticipated, requiring many high-precision compound angles. I worked through these issues by trying out multiple approaches using various jigs, but ultimately relied on much trial and error. Another issue that I had as a result of this difficulty was tolerance. I was easily able to get five pieces together, but ultimately the 20th would be quite a bit off and on a different plane, and I would have to rip it all apart or try to custom fit a piece. Finally, it was a challenge finding a way to replace each light bulb. I realized that I would need to use each dodecahedron as a light shade and have it be removable. In between each dodecahedron, I made a flange in order to keep each unit from spinning or falling off.

Did you use any special equipment or software?

I used SketchUp and SolidWorks as my 3D CAD software.

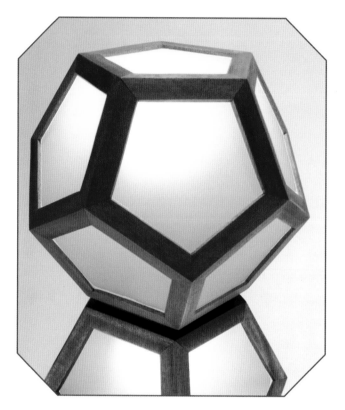

DIMENSIONS: 62" H x 12.5" W x 12.5" D
WEIGHT: 15 lb.
MATERIALS: Mahogany, steel
FINISH: Tung oil

2021
2ND
PLACE

OUTDOOR FURNITURE

ASHLEY WONG

MARK KEPPEL HIGH SCHOOL | INSTRUCTOR: CUONG LAM

What was your inspiration for this piece?

This piece was a reproduction; I intentionally scaled it to 1/8th of its actual size since I had no machinery at home to cut the wood had it not been scaled.

What were your project goals?

My project goal was for the pieces to be flush as possible with no gaps.

What challenges did you encounter?

As I was gluing the walls, I noticed that the height was uneven. However, I was able to fix it by sanding down the top so it was flat when I placed the top miter cuts.

Did you use any special equipment or software?

I used SketchUp to model my project before starting construction.

DIMENSIONS: 3″ H x 3″ W x 3″ D

WEIGHT: 0.1 lb.

MATERIALS: Poplar

FINISH: None

2019
2ND PLACE

HARD NINETY

COLE DANIELS

ROLLA TECHNICAL INSTITUTE | INSTRUCTOR: ROBERT STUDDARD

What was your inspiration for this piece?

I was interested in the idea of a shuffleboard table, but with minimum floor space and the regulation size stretching 22´ long, I knew I had to be creative. I started sketching different shapes and sizes, and eventually found a gentleman online who was custom-producing corner shuffleboard tables, which inspired me further.

What were your project goals?
Did you use any unique construction methods?

My main goal was to build my project to the best of my potential. My other goal was to make the project have a unique style and flair.

What challenges did you encounter?

One of the main challenges was making sure my panels were glued up at a perfect right angle. I was able to overcome this by clamping down framing squares onto the work table and gluing my joints adjacent to the square. The legs were cut individually, so making sure all six legs were identical was another challenge. Also, building the box perfectly square so that the playing surface fit inside of it properly was another challenge.

Did you use any special equipment or software?

I used a Unique door machine to cut all of my stiles and rails for the panels. The panels were made using veneer that I glued in a vacuum bag. The shuffle board playing surface was designed with woodWop software. The shape, inlays, miter, and the counter top bolt slots were all cut on a Weeke CNC router.

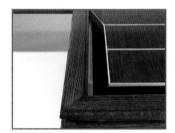

DIMENSIONS: 34″ H x 78″ W x 78″ D

WEIGHT: 300 lb.

MATERIALS: Oak, maple, curly maple (veneer), BauBuche, particle board

FINISH: Red mahogany stain, ML Campbell MagnaMax (semi-gloss)

CHIKUU TOU SORA

WALTER EMANN

PRINCETON DAY SCHOOL | INSTRUCTOR: CHRIS MAHER

2017
2ND
PLACE

What was your inspiration for this piece?

I've always been a fan of traditional Japanese architecture and design; the way it flows so smoothly, but remains crisp along the edges. It's a majestic art form that truly embodies effort, intricacy, and complexity. This piece called on my ability to employ careful techniques and ornamental styles in an attempt to produce a piece that reimagined Japanese design in a slightly simplified sense.

What were your project goals?

One of my main goals was to utilize many hand-cut joints, as do many traditional Japanese pieces. Where applicable, I made sure to put my chisel to the wood. Even though it's not really visible, I believe that it's really a mark of true craftsmanship and shows dedication to the design process.

What challenges did you encounter?

Cutting the rice paper to the correct length, cutting the slots for the wooden strips, and then physically fitting the rice paper with said strips certainly proved to be very challenging. Not only that, but I ensured that each panel of the lamp shade is fully replaceable. I spent the better half of a day preparing the paper and setting it in its final place. It required a very dexterous hand and a very, very patient mind.

Did you use any special equipment or software?

I modeled some parts of the project using the SketchUp design program.

DIMENSIONS: 60″ H x 12″ W x 12″ D

WEIGHT: 15 lb.

MATERIALS: Black walnut, cherry, mahogany

FINISH: Tung oil

NESTED CONSOLE TABLES

JENNY HEFFERAN

MADISON COLLEGE | INSTRUCTOR: PATRICK MOLZAHN

What was your inspiration for this piece?

My interest in space-saving design and multi-functional furniture inspired this set of tables. For my rental apartment, I wanted two console tables with drawers. Since I don't know the layout of my next home, I wanted to build something that was flexible. As a result, I designed the console tables such that they can nest and function as one piece of furniture, if needed. This reduces the footprint of the tables and increases the likelihood I will be able to find space for them in my next home.

What were your project goals?

My project goal was to build space-saving nesting console tables that would look beautiful either when nested together or apart.

What challenges did you encounter?

The placement of the drawer pulls was a particular challenge. Some placements looked great with the tables nested, but looked unbalanced when apart, or vice versa. I considered many options and the placement became a key design element for the set. As a beginner woodworker, I made numerous mistakes during construction. I am grateful that this project taught me how many woodworking mistakes can be easily fixed without sacrificing the aesthetics of the final product.

Did you use any special equipment or software?

Since my days in the woodshop were limited to accommodate social distancing, I decided to learn and use ALPHACAM to cut the plywood parts using the CNC router. This allowed me to program the parts from home and helped me complete the project within the limited shop time. Since I had four drawers to install, I made a simple jig to assist with the drawer runner installation (my first time creating such a jig).

DIMENSIONS: 33″ H x 48″ W x 12″ D

WEIGHT: 102 lb.

MATERIALS: Baltic birch plywood, mahogany, soft maple

FINISH: Pre-catalyzed lacquer

DETACH
VALERIE ALT
CALIFORNIA COLLEGE OF THE ARTS | INSTRUCTOR: RUSSELL BALDON

What was your inspiration for this piece?
When moving to the United States from Germany, I was overwhelmed with all the technology and lights that surrounded me in my day-to-day life all of a sudden. I took the exact measurements from an iPhone 4S and made it ten times bigger, making a precise but nonfunctional iPhone as a coffee table to play board games on.

What were your project goals?
I wanted to attract people and spike their interest in this gigantic iPhone table.

What challenges did you encounter?
It was difficult to simplify something so perfect and to reduce the object to just the features necessary to make it authentic and recognizable.

DIMENSIONS: 17″ H x 23″ W x 48″ D
WEIGHT: 60 lb.
MATERIALS: Plywood veneered with maple and walnut, LED lights

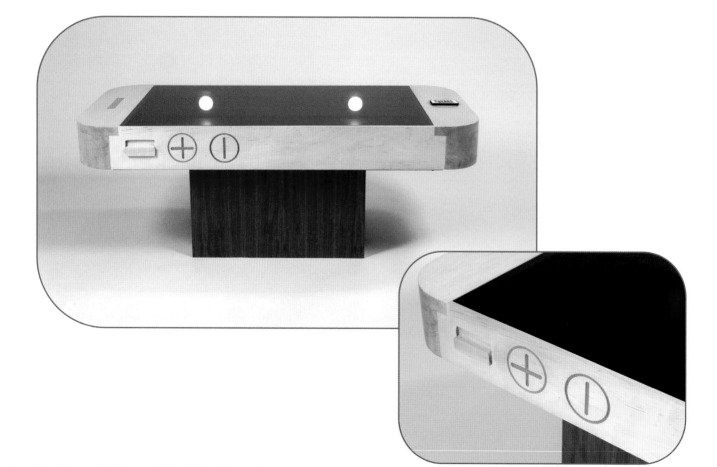

2017
1ST
PLACE

SCYTHE

WILLIAM STRENGER

PALOMAR COLLEGE | INSTRUCTOR: JENNIFER ANDERSON

What was your inspiration for this piece?

As part of a design class, I was tasked with developing a design based on a concept. I envisioned ideas dropping out of a nebulous gray cloud like rain or hail, with some captured and concentrated with others. Developing this further, I ended up with the shape of a tapered funnel. Curved components from the funnel shape resulted in the general profile of the lamp base and the repeating shapes on the lampshade.

What were your project goals?

I had never done a sculpted piece and wanted to experiment with various shaping techniques, as well as incorporate brass into the design. The final piece also needed to blend with the design of a casual Mid-Century chair I had previously made, as well as provide a functional light source for reading.

What challenges did you encounter?

I needed to operate the lamp while seated, so conventional switches either wouldn't work or would be unsightly. Adding a brass inlay into the spine of the lamp created a touch dimmer. Shaping and inlaying the brass proved to be challenging. While shaping and finishing, care had to be taken as not to contaminate the walnut with brass filings.

Did you use any special equipment or software?

Gross shaping of the lamp body was done with a right-angle grinder and carbide shaping disc. Fine tuning was done with spokeshaves, rasps, and sandpaper. Channels for the wiring and brass spine were made with a router following a pattern I made from MDF. The shade used a top turned from solid piece of walnut and a ring turned from segmented walnut. The tapered walnut pieces were hand-shaped.

DIMENSIONS: 51″ H x 27″ W x 9″ D
WEIGHT: 11 lb.
MATERIALS: Walnut, brass, movingui veneer laminated to thin plastic
FINISH: Liberon Finishing Oil, Liberon Black Bison Wax Polish, nitrocellulose lacquer

AND THE RABBIT JUMPED OVER THE MOON

MADELAINE NELSON

SELKIRK COLLEGE | INSTRUCTOR: DAVID RINGHEIM

2021

2ND PLACE

What was your inspiration for this piece?

The marquetry design was inspired by my niece. Moving away from her and my home to attend this school was very emotional. I associate her with rabbits (her favorite stuffed animal is a bunny); I have tattoos of the moon. The design combines symbols associated with the both of us. Though the idea of a rabbit jumping over the moon is obviously impossible, it feels like I could do the impossible to be with her again.

What were your project goals?
Did you use any unique construction methods?

My immediate goal was to make a dovetail project for school. The project was entirely done with hand tools except for bandsawing off the top. I planed, sawed, cut the dovetails, and more by hand.

What challenges did you encounter?

I encountered the usual challenges associated with hand tools and first-time dovetail making. I solved these problems with patience and practice.

Did you use any special equipment or software?

The most specialized tool I used was a chevalet to cut the marquetry.

DIMENSIONS: 4″ H x 9.5″ W x 7″ D
WEIGHT: 5 lb.
MATERIALS: Cherry, chatoyant arbutus, assorted other species

GAME TABLE

RYAN TIRRELL

BRIGHAM YOUNG UNIVERSITY | INSTRUCTOR: TIMOTHY McNEILL

2019
2ND
PLACE

What was your inspiration for this piece?

I wanted to create a game table that would be seen uniquely as a game table. For inspiration, I saw a coffee table made by a former hockey player out of his game sticks. The sticks making up the top of the table inspired me to use game boxes to create a game table.

What were your project goals?
Did you use any unique construction methods?

The goal was to incorporate game boxes into the construction. In order to preserve them, I coated them in Mod Podge before laminating them down to the tabletop. Once the table was laminated, I poured tabletop resin over the games to level the tabletop while sealing in the games.

What challenges did you encounter?

During a larger pour, there was a problem with the resin curing correctly, resulting in a gummy and rubbery finish. It took a bit of removing, re-sanding, and refilling to remedy the situation. Once refinished, I sprayed it with a lacquer.

Did you use any special equipment or software?

Tabletop resin was an essential part and a new experience for me. It proved to be the most challenging part of the table.

DIMENSIONS: 42″ H x 48″ W x 48″ D
WEIGHT: 150 lb.
MATERIALS: Solid walnut, walnut plywood, Baltic birch plywood, resin
FINISH: Sprayed lacquer clear coat, Danish oil, beeswax and mineral oil mix

CANVAS
JIALUN XIONG
ART CENTER COLLEGE OF DESIGN | INSTRUCTOR: PENNY HERSCOVITCH

What was your inspiration for this piece?

My concept for this lighting design was a carefully curated landscape story created by texture, light, and negative space. I wanted to create a modern hanging art piece. I was also inspired by the positive and negative space created by light and textures.

What were your project goals?
Did you use any unique construction methods?

I really wanted a handcrafted feeling on the piece, so I used a very traditional Japanese woodburning technique to treat the wood. Repeating the steps of burning and wire brushing naturally brought out the wood grain to create a rich texture and charcoal color on the surface.

What challenges did you encounter?

It was really hard to hide the light source and light up the textured surface at the same time. The angle was really tricky. Because this lighting was designed in two pieces, I raised one piece up and also made the whole piece concave.

Did you use any special equipment or software?

It was my first time using a torch.

DIMENSIONS: 20″ H x 17″ W x 0.5″ D
WEIGHT: 10 lb.
MATERIALS: Western red cedar
FINISH: Charcoal spray

HIGH SCHOOL

POST-SECONDARY

TABLES

This is one of the more popular categories in the contest! To enter, a piece must serve as some kind of stand or table, including occasional tables, gaming tables, coffee tables, or dining tables. Emphasis during judging is on design integrity, craftsmanship, joinery, and aesthetics.

QUEEN ANNE TILT-TOP PIE CRUST TABLE

WYATT THALLER

BENZIE CENTRAL HIGH SCHOOL | INSTRUCTOR: DAVID BARRESI

2021
1ST
PLACE

What was your inspiration for this piece?

My inspiration was a Queen Anne–style tilt-top table that my dad made for my grandmother. My family all loved that piece. The table went missing, and my sister was heartbroken. Given the chance to make a table in my furniture-making class, I told her I'd make a table like dad's that she could keep forever.

What were your project goals?
Did you use any unique construction methods?

My goal was to create a family heirloom. I had never done any real woodworking before this piece, so my goal was to listen, learn, and try all the new tools and machines. I used a unique process making the pie crust. I glued a mitered frame on the tabletop instead of digging it out.

What challenges did you encounter?

The biggest challenge was making the pie crust. I had to miter 12 different pieces together, but the inside edge would constantly catch on the router. I had to make a total of 38 pieces until I had a perfect set. Then, I had to trim each piece multiple times to get the miters to fit perfectly.

Did you use any special equipment or software?

I used a lathe to turn the pedestal and a bandsaw to cut the legs and pie crust. The only hardware used is the tilt-top table latch.

DIMENSIONS: 18″ H x 27″ W x 43″ D
WEIGHT: 17 lb.
MATERIALS: Cherry
FINISH: Cherry stain, lacquer

VISIONS OF RHYTHM
SPENCER JOHNSON

CORNER CANYON HIGH SCHOOL | INSTRUCTOR: TIMOTHY McNEILL

What was your inspiration for this piece?

Thomas Moser's American Bungalow Table was the primary influence for this particular design. Several details have been changed to make this piece original and unique.

What were your project goals?
Did you use any unique construction methods?

A one-of-a-kind, high-end Craftsman table was the overall goal for this project. This table is a dining room statement, designed to couple functionality with beauty. Unique glass tri-panels in the tabletop create windows that display the intricate framework of the base. This table is a contemporary take on a classic style of American furniture, featuring reverse-tapered legs and Craftsman-style shaping on corners and edges. No hardware or fasteners were used. Strong joints were chosen to ensure daily functionality and stability: half laps and dados to join the stretchers and aprons, mortise-and-tenons to join stretchers and legs, and dowels to join stiles and rails of the tabletop framework. The base of the table is secured to the tabletop with dowels. All joinery is tight, providing structurally solid construction and a clean look.

What challenges did you encounter?

My original design featured a solid cherry tabletop. The boards I selected were extremely twisted. While gluing the top together, I alternated twists with the hope of yielding a flat surface. Although it was pretty, the tabletop was simply far too warped to use. After hours of brainstorming, I finally came up with the perfect tabletop: a beautiful cherry frame featuring three glass panels that perfectly displayed the framework underneath and added to the overall elegance of the table. Further, a tolerance of 1/8″ is the custom glass industry standard, which meant the framework, with its 1/16″ reveal, could not be assembled prior to receiving the glass. Another challenge was keeping the legs perfectly square while creating the reverse taper.

DIMENSIONS: 30″ H x 42″ W x 72″ D
WEIGHT: 120 lb.
MATERIALS: FAS (first and second grade) cherry, glass
FINISH: Linseed oil

CHERRY BLAWESOME

MATTHEW SHIPLETT

CEDAR RIDGE HIGH SCHOOL | INSTRUCTOR: KEITH YOW

2017
1ST
PLACE

What was your inspiration for this piece?

During design, I was primarily inspired by traditional Japanese woodworking joints. I also found additional inspiration in Kiyosi Seike's book, *The Art of Japanese Joinery,* which mentions the interwoven connection and respect that wood and woodworkers share in the designing of furniture and structures.

What were your project goals?
Did you use any unique construction methods?

My project goal was to create something original while bringing innovation to a traditional technique. This led to a table that would reflect historical Japanese techniques by applying modern construction methods. Another important goal was to create depth in the illusion of the interwoven pattern. This was accomplished through shaded veneers for the tabletop and required the unique method of shading the veneer with hot sand—a technique Japanese craftsmen have used for centuries.

What challenges did you encounter?

I would say that every element of this table was a challenge. First, I needed to do in-depth research to learn about the techniques and styles of my design. Also, this was my first experience with the tusk tenon joint and I wanted to create a triple-tusk tenon rather than the commonly used single tenon. With over 600 pieces of veneer used, the marquetry was time consuming, as was the shading technique to create the illusion of a shadow on each "woven" segment. Finally, it was a challenge to fit both the apron's woven half-lapped joints and the tusk tenon. Fluctuations of the maple used in my woven section became hard to deal with as seasons—and humidity—changed. And, the triple-tusk tenons required a large amount of trigonometry to determine the size of each tusk hole in order to fit the tusk with even pressure throughout the joint.

Did you use any special equipment or software?

To uniformly cut the veneer, I used a carbon-dioxide fueled laser engraver.

DIMENSIONS: 33″ H x 45″ W x 15″ D

WEIGHT: 25 lb.

MATERIALS: Cherry, maple, African ceiba; walnut burl, maple (veneers)

FINISH: Formby's Furniture Workshop Traditional Tung Oil Finish, beeswax and pure tung oil mix

CONTEMPORARY TABLE

JACOB FARNSWORTH

CORNER CANYON HIGH SCHOOL | INSTRUCTOR: TIMOTHY McNEILL

2021
2ND
PLACE

What was your inspiration for this piece?

This was my final senior project and I wanted to incorporate everything that I had learned, while continuing to push my limits. I came up with the idea of having one board that splits and curves in opposite directions.

What were your project goals?
Did you use any unique construction methods?

My goal was to make a table with curves and difficult joinery. To do the difficult curves on the top of the piece, I had to learn and use a vacuum clamp to glue the curve down tight enough.

What challenges did you encounter?

In my original design, I had just a single rail connecting the two halves of the piece; after making a mock-up, I realized this would not be strong enough to hold it together. After much thought, I added the three rosewood tenons to connect the two sides. The bends and angles were also difficult, but by double-checking many times and measuring, it was able to work out. Last, when I glued one of the through tenons into the top of the table and used the mallet to press the wedge/joint into place, the entire top of the curved stile split and shattered. I was worried it was too far gone, but using a lot of clamps, glue, and sanding, I was able to make it look as it had before, while maintaining the strength of the joint.

DIMENSIONS: 35″ H x 44″ W x 15″ D
WEIGHT: 21 lb.
MATERIALS: Cherry, rosewood
FINISH: Linseed oil

ZARYCHA SAFARI

ZACK HOLT

MUSTANG HIGH SCHOOL | INSTRUCTOR: MIKE McGARRY

What was your inspiration for this piece?

A picture of a desk online similar to this was my inspiration. I fell in love with the lines, curves, and design elements. I knew it would be a difficult piece to recreate, but I did not intend on making an exact duplicate, and I wanted to challenge myself.

What were your project goals?

My project goal was to construct not only a conversation piece, but to also build a fully functional desk. I wanted the design of it and the variations of wood types to stand out versus other desks.

What challenges did you encounter?

I anticipated that the sides of my desk, made with a plywood sheet, would be pliable enough to bend and manipulate, but that was not the case; I needed to spend quite a bit of additional time cutting dadoes into the entire width of the sides. Also, I did not expect to put so many hours into handplaning the curly maple legs.

Did you use any special equipment or software?

It was my first time using the vintage router plane and the vacuum bag pressing system for my veneer work.

DIMENSIONS: 30″ H x 66″ W x 24″ D
WEIGHT: 80 lb.
MATERIALS: Maple plywood, walnut, curly maple, sapele (veneer)
FINISH: Gloss lacquer

TRIPLE HELIX
SPENCER JOHNSON
CORNER CANYON HIGH SCHOOL | INSTRUCTOR: TIMOTHY McNEILL

2017
2ND
PLACE

What was your inspiration for this piece?
In the process of brainstorming for inspiration to build a table, I stumbled across a picture of a bentwood coffee table made by a classmate. The table featured three legs that grew in diameter as they spiraled upward toward the piece of glass they supported. The shape of the legs was something I had never seen before in the context of woodworking.

What were your project goals?
Did you use any unique construction methods?
My overall goal for this project was to create a unique and visually appealing table for people to use and admire. Moreover, I aimed to enhance my understanding and ability in form and mold construction, as well as bent lamination. Another objective was to increase my ability to produce strong and precise joinery.

What challenges did you encounter?
Creating the mold for bending the legs was a challenge in itself. A great deal of time and effort went into the design and construction of the mold and it was the most difficult aspect of building the table. Due to the complex and abstract shape of the legs, sanding and shaping was difficult. Achieving the consistent round over on all edges was the most difficult part of shaping the legs. Also, the curvature of the legs combined with the disc shape of the center piece made for a difficult joint to cut.

Did you use any special equipment or software?
The center discs were cut out using a CNC machine. I created and used a jig that served the purpose of ensuring consistent positioning of the legs in relation to the center piece.

DIMENSIONS: 24″ H x 40″ W x 40″ D
WEIGHT: 38.5 lb.
MATERIALS: Cherry, FAS (first and second grade) walnut, glass
FINISH: Linseed oil

HONESTLY ELEGANT

MATTHEW STEGER

DAKOTA HIGH SCHOOL | INSTRUCTOR: CHAD CAMPAU

What was your inspiration for this piece?

I was influenced by a company that produces this type of piece, but the overall design came from my desire to make a table that looks like it came from a custom furniture design manufacturer. I wanted to limit structural elements and feature elegant shapes. This design has formality, but a modest support structure, so attention can be focused on the table surface.

What were your project goals?
Did you use any unique construction methods?

There were several personal goals: to design a museum-quality piece that could serve as a focal point of any home; to use exotic materials; and to learn new and different ways to build furniture.

What challenges did you encounter?

The careful and somewhat tedious step-by-step process of working with exotic veneer, like ebony and burl walnut, was challenging and educational. So, too, was my first time working with an MDF core.

Did you use any special equipment or software?

Laser technology was used to cut veneer strips along with the burl squares for a perfect book match. A CNC was used to make the curved pieces for the leg assembly to insure uniform parts. All laser and CNC parts were created with design software.

DIMENSIONS: 29″ H x 48″ W x 72″ D

WEIGHT: 175 lb.

MATERIALS: MDF; walnut burl, ebony, curly maple (veneers)

FINISH: Sprayed conversion lacquer

THE KLEIN TABLE

WALTER EMANN

PRINCETON DAY SCHOOL | INSTRUCTOR: CHRIS MAHER

2019

F

FINALIST

What was your inspiration for this piece?

I've always been into working with live edge. I also tend towards crisp and interesting geometry. So, when one of my oldest friends gave me this really cool slab of ash, right away I knew I wanted to do something crazy with it and dedicate it to him. Thanks for the wood, Chris Klein!

What were your project goals?
Did you use any unique construction methods?

In addition to honoring Chris with this piece, I wanted to make something to give to my brother and my parents before I went to college. I took the big ash slab and cut it in two and thought, why not put the live edge on the inside of the table? Then I stuck it on top of some weird angles and threw a circle into the whole thing.

What challenges did you encounter?

When routing out the ash to make room for the walnut circle, my jig ended up extending a bit here and there, so I sanded different places down on the walnut circle so that both it and the accents could fit. I kept playing around with it, and it came out much better than I'd hoped. My threaded inserts also kept stripping before I could get them as far into the ash as they needed to go, so I was left with exposed stripped metal to file off.

Did you use any special equipment or software?

Steam bending the black oak for the accents around the circle involved steaming equipment, clamps, and jigs for keeping the shape.

DIMENSIONS: 15" H x 22" W x 40" D
WEIGHT: 30 lb.
MATERIALS: Ash, walnut, black oak
FINISH: Tung oil/mineral spirits/polyurethane mix

MID-CENTURY MODERN COFFEE TABLE

KATJA PEEREBOOM

CEDAR RIDGE HIGH SCHOOL | INSTRUCTOR: KEITH YOW

What was your inspiration for this piece?

My inspiration was Mid-Century Modern furniture. I really like the design and how different it is from most of the furniture I encounter on a daily basis.

What were your project goals? Did you use any unique construction methods?

My goal was to create a functional and creative coffee table for my home. To give the table more of a Mid-Century vibe, I divided the inside unevenly and included only one drawer. This gave the table an unexpected look and added negative space to the design.

What challenges did you encounter?

There were challenges with the biscuit jointer, which left some unplanned holes in the table. I concealed the imperfections with several inlays, which added to the overall design and visual interest. Also, the half-blind dovetails on the drawer were my first attempt at a dovetail joint of any sort.

Did you use any special equipment or software?

For the first time, I used a laser to cut all of the veneer. I also used a jig on the bandsaw to create the tails of my dovetail joints.

DIMENSIONS: 18″ H x 43″ W x 19″ D
WEIGHT: 44 lb.
MATERIALS: Walnut, poplar; birdseye maple, riftsawn maple (veneers)
FINISH: Minwax Polycrylic (gloss)

DIMENSIONS

BAYLOR BRUCE

MUSTANG HIGH SCHOOL | INSTRUCTOR: MIKE McGARRY

What was your inspiration for this piece?

My inspiration was to create an infinity feel. I want the viewer to feel that you can reach into the middle of this piece and get lost in it. I love taking basic woodworking and putting a crazy spin on it.

Did you use any unique construction methods?

The top is laminated and composed of four different types of wood. The bottom is made of three trapezoids all laminated into three pieces.

What challenges did you encounter?

I originally found this pattern in the form of a small cutting board, but during the construction I noticed that the original designer had messed up, so I had to figure out how the actual flow of this pattern worked. Another of the main problems was that all the pieces were too small to be cut safely on the table saw, so I had to create a jig that clamped each individual piece down.

Did you use any special equipment or software?

I used a vacuum press to laminate all the bottom pieces to the table.

DIMENSIONS: 20" H x 48" W x 24" D

WEIGHT: 70 lb.

MATERIALS: Maple, purpleheart, ebony, padauk

FINISH: Semi-gloss lacquer

FLYING TABLE

JINSOO KIM

CENTER FOR FURNITURE CRAFTSMANSHIP | INSTRUCTOR: TIM ROUSSEAU

2021
1ST
PLACE

What was your inspiration for this piece?

This piece was a school project in curvature; the inspiration was
to make a 3D curved shape expressing wood's free nature.

What were your project goals?
Did you use any unique construction methods?

The project goal was to make a very unique table through learning and
training skills in bending wood. The 3D curved lower tabletop is a unique
element of this project. I coopered steam-bent staves to create it. The
upper flat tabletop contrasts, but harmonizes, by adding conventional
"normal" table function. To minimize any dents occurring in the steam
bending of the turned legs, special bending and drying forms were created.

What challenges did you encounter?

For the steam bending and the shaping of 54″ x 2″ x 3/4″ staves
for the curved tabletop, several durable, accurate, and efficient
jigs were made. For the accurate boring of the two tabletops, the
best way was to drill angled mortise holes together with a jig.

Did you use any special equipment or software?

The CNC was used to make templates for all the jigs,
and the Rhino program for 3D modeling.

DIMENSIONS: 30″ H x 50″ W x 28″ D

WEIGHT: 50 lb.

MATERIALS: Maple, birdseye maple, poplar

FINISH: Murdoch's (Hard Sealer, Hard Oil), shellac

NAUTICAL MARQUETRY TABLE

NICHOLAS MARALDO

THE FURNITURE INSTITUTE OF MASSACHUSETTS | INSTRUCTOR: PHILIP C. LOWE

2019
1ST
PLACE

What was your inspiration for this piece?

This serpentine table is an interpretation of a period piece in the Federal style. I've modernized and embellished it with a nautical theme to celebrate my time as a Navy sailor and subsequent residence on the North Shore of Massachusetts. The anchors frame the piece, and the center compass rose inlay is set into a walnut burl that is reminiscent of a nautical map.

What were your project goals?
Did you use any unique construction methods?

My project goal was to maximize my learning experience, so I decided to design a piece that incorporated as many different woodworking elements as possible. I practiced veneering curved and flat surfaces, hammer veneering, marquetry, inlay, producing highly stylized bellflowers, sand shading, cutting veneers from solid stock, crossbanding and stringing, spandrel corner inlay, making banding for inlay, and shaping curved drawers with cockbeading.

What challenges did you encounter?

This table had many curved surfaces that were tricky to join and veneer. Highly stylized bellflowers took a lot of practice to get right in both cutting and shading. Banding was a complex endeavor, as tolerances were very tight and creating curved sections required precision. I found that a good pair of dial calipers and careful thicknessing of materials was key, as small errors tend to compound exponentially over each step.

DIMENSIONS: 31″ H x 39″ W x 15.125″ D
WEIGHT: 10 lb.
MATERIALS: Mahogany (solid, veneer), eastern white pine; walnut burl, holly, Gaboon ebony (veneers)
FINISH: Blond shellac, clear paste wax

Did you use any special equipment or software?

I made my own veneer hammer, an angled shooting board for the banding, and several scratch stocks to cut the areas for inlay. I also used hot hide glue for both the joinery and veneering.

AZULEJOS TABLE

CODY CAMPANIE

SEATTLE CENTRAL COLLEGE | INSTRUCTOR: JEFFREY WASSERMAN

2017 1ST PLACE

What was your inspiration for this piece?

The overall dimensions of the table were designed according to proportions of the golden ratio, with both the plan and side elevation rendered as a 16" x 42" rectangle. The form and structure of the legs and aprons drew influence from Scandinavian sofa tables of the 1950s. Specifically, the subtle curve of the apron pays homage to Folke Ohlsson, while the top edge detail references Finn Juhl. The top veneer pattern is inspired by *azulejos*, the glazed tiling of Moorish influence found throughout Portugal.

What were your project goals?

The goals of this project were to highlight the beauty of teak and to show complex geometry expressed by simply altering grain direction. The organic modernism of the base structure is meant to appear clean, light, and honest in its showcasing of traditional joinery.

What challenges did you encounter?

The biggest design and construction challenge was sequencing the procedures and assembly. To express details such as the veneer extension to the tabletop edge, while maintaining a solid wood edge, the order of operations required great consideration.

Did you use any special equipment or software?

This table was my first foray into the challenging yet gratifying art of veneering. The individual pieces of veneer for the top pattern were hand cut on a Virutex mitering cutter. Additionally, the mortises of the leg and apron joinery were cut using a horizontal boring mortiser.

DIMENSIONS: 16" H x 42" W x 16" D

WEIGHT: 18 lb.

MATERIALS: Teak (solid, veneer), industrial-grade particle board

FINISH: Skidmore's Liquid Beeswax Woodfinish

ZIG-ZAG STARDUST COFFEE TABLE

ALEASHA CARR

SELKIRK COLLEGE | INSTRUCTOR: SCOTT STEVENS

2021
2ND PLACE

What was your inspiration for this piece?

Angles ended up being the main theme of the design: the stark angles of the carcase; the mellower angle used in the front/back parquetry; the drawer pull; the little angled parquetry stars; and I even used dovetails instead of box joints in the drawer construction. Inspiration for the decoration of the table came from the designer Nada Debs. Her work frequently incorporates patterns and also makes use of marquetry inlays in the face of pieces, sometimes intersecting the two.

What were your project goals?

I am very interested in exploring different veneering techniques. I had tried marquetry in the fall semester and wanted to design something more geometric that would be conducive to a parquetry design.

What challenges did you encounter?

The construction challenge that I got hung up on was figuring out a clamping system for glue-up. The initial cauls were overbuilt, obscured the glue joint, and didn't apply pressure where needed. So I simplified. Small blocks with the profiles of the top and bottom edges cut into them allowed the glue joint to be visible and gave me greater ability to adjust the pressure of the clamps where needed.

Did you use any special equipment or software?

I used SketchUp throughout the design and building process. It sped up the task of figuring out the spacing for the chevron parquetry pattern and helped make sense of the intersections of angles, while giving accurate dimensions to cut to for the construction of the carcase. I also set up a jig to hand cut consistent strips for the parquetry, and became acquainted with the Domino cutter.

DIMENSIONS: 16″ H x 47″ W x 26″ D

WEIGHT: 75 lb.

MATERIALS: African mahogany (solid, veneer), hard maple, Baltic birch plywood; curly maple, hemlock (veneers)

FINISH: Osmo TopOil

CONVEX DESK
CHRISTOPHER MERCHANT
CENTER FOR FURNITURE CRAFTSMANSHIP | INSTRUCTOR: ALED LEWIS

What was your inspiration for this piece?
The inspiration for this piece came from minimalist design. The goal was to create a table in which all the components are visually independent of each other while still forming a strong structure. The architecture of the Sistine Chapel inspired the structure of the desk; both the table and the desk use connections between domed and planar elements to create rigid structure.

What were your project goals?
Did you use any unique construction methods?
This project was meant as an exploration of curvature techniques in woodworking, so I incorporated both steam bending and coopering into the design and construction of the piece. I steam bent the staves for the coopered form underneath the flat table top. The bent pieces were then shaped into their final coopered forms using a shaper jig to finalize their thickness and a planer sled to apply the angles to their edges. My desire to incorporate these techniques in construction led me to the unique design element of the domed surface beneath the flat top.

What challenges did you encounter?
The biggest challenge I faced was in creating the offset angles for the turned blocks between the top and domed surface beneath. I turned blocks to the appropriate diameter with a hole bored for a round tenon, then determined the top and bottom angles and their offset from a detailed 3D model. I created a jig for a crosscut table saw with a protruding dowel that fit the bored hold snugly. The turned blocks were fastened to the dowel with a shallow screw and were presented to the angled table saw blade once on each end. Between cuts, the block is turned around and rotated to provide the necessary rotational offset between the angled cuts.

DIMENSIONS: 29″ H x 47″ W x 26″ D
WEIGHT: 50 lb.
MATERIALS: Ash
FINISH: Osmo

WRITING TABLE
SCOTT STEVENS

SELKIRK COLLEGE | INSTRUCTOR: DAVID RINGHEIM

2017
2ND
PLACE

What was your inspiration for this piece?

The table is a gift for my sister. The curved aspects were inspired by Art Nouveau stylings, while the raised rear cubby section was a take on Mid-Century Modern Danish. I blended the two styles together by adding a solid border around the perimeter of the table that also follows the shape of the cubby section, thereby adding a style consistent with Victorian-era design.

What were your project goals?
Did you use any unique construction methods?

A major goal of this piece was to challenge my skill set in wood bending and joinery onto curved surfaces. Dovetails were used to attach the front top rail to the side rails and front legs, while mortise-and-tenon joinery was used to assemble the remaining table frame. The four drawers were assembled with hand-cut half-blind dovetails. For wood bending, the front was the focal piece of the project, repeating and transitioning from the front edge of the tabletop through to the drawers and on to the veneered border and raised cubby section. Even the drawer pulls, a lamination of figured anigre veneer, were pressed to follow the curve of the drawer.

DIMENSIONS: 34″ H x 36″ W x 24″ D
WEIGHT: 70 lb.
MATERIALS: Black walnut, hard maple, MDF, figured anigre (veneer)
FINISH: Post-catalyzed lacquer

What challenges did you encounter?

In order to maintain a consistent curve along the front of the table, the two front legs required an angled front face to match the shape of the adjacent drawer front. The joinery connecting the drawer sides to the curved drawer front required angled half-blind dovetails hand cut into the drawer front. The cubby itself has two unique curves on the front face: horizontal and vertical.

Did you use any special equipment or software?

I used SketchUp for the drafting process and jig designs, and BobCAD-CAM and a CNC machine for cutting jigs.

THE TRUMAN TABLE

SHAUN BELLIVEAU-THOMPSON

SELKIRK COLLEGE | INSTRUCTOR: DAVID RINGHEIM

2021
HM
HONORABLE
MENTION

What was your inspiration for this piece?

My original inspiration for this piece was a hologram or incomplete render of a generated "world" that has mapped out the borders in grid form with the facade layer being generated after a slight delay. I had hoped to portray that the boundaries of the table interior and the plant life within were somehow computer generated. I have also designed the drawer pull to be a shelf, although quite simple in construction; this leaves the user feeling like this hidden feature has a certain advanced quality, contributing to the feel of futuristic technology.

What were your project goals?
Did you use any unique construction methods?

My goals for this project were to design something unique, as well as challenge myself with physical construction. I hope for this piece to be an eye catcher for potential clients.

What challenges did you encounter?

As my design came to fruition, I felt the original leg design was not as aesthetically pleasing. I was left looking for something bold enough to match the overall appearance of the table, while still fitting the allure I was attempting to create. In construction, the lattice had some gaps along a few edges; I edge-banded with the same board of mahogany to fill the gaps. By far the largest challenge (or oversight) was the stain. On my third coat, I worked the stain for too long and it began to set up, pulling fibers from the applicator rag. This resulted in sanding the entire oak carcass back to bare. Although this was a huge setback, I am incredibly pleased with how the finish came out afterward.

Did you use any special equipment or software?

The project was designed using SketchUp Pro.

DIMENSIONS: 17" H x 24" W x 59" D
WEIGHT: 80 lb.
MATERIALS: African mahogany, Pro-Core white oak plywood, rare earth magnets
FINISH: Osmo Oil Stain (Silver Gray), Osmo TopOil

CUBAN MAHOGANY NIGHT STANDS

JOSHUA STERNS

THE KRENOV SCHOOL | INSTRUCTOR: LAURA MAYS

2019
HM
HONORABLE MENTION

What was your inspiration for this piece?

My inspiration was a classic Shaker design, but with the addition of non-Shaker curved laminations and veneering. The straightforward Shaker design mixes well with many furniture styles, particularly modern ones, which keeps them from looking dated. Creating pieces that are useful and beautiful and can be passed down over generations rather than discarded for the next new thing is always a driving theme for me.

What were your project goals?
Did you use any unique construction methods?

In conforming the Shaker inspiration toward my own style, the first goal was to make the construction more challenging without resorting to gimmicks or unnecessary complexity. Adding curves was a first step. The second goal was to select a distinctive wood without overpowering the simple feel of the tables. This was solved with a small piece of Cuban mahogany with an interesting backstory involving Hurricane Andrew. I managed to slice just enough veneers for the project and it helped achieve a balance between design and materials.

What challenges did you encounter?

Starting a project with the exact amount of wood needed is a terrible idea, but it was unavoidable. I spent more time than usual planning each step, as any serious mistake could be unfixable. Because the grain of the Cuban mahogany was prone to chipping out in the planer, I found a local shop with a wide belt sander to rent. Also, as the fronts of the tables are curved, curved-edge banding had to be attached to the curved top and bottom shelf.

Did you use any special equipment or software?

The brass pulls on the drawer fronts were the first metal work I've done. This was also the first time I used a vacuum bag for gluing the veneers to the substrates.

DIMENSIONS: 22″ H x 14″ W x 18″ D

WEIGHT: 35 lb.

MATERIALS: ApplePly, Cuban mahogany (veneer), doussie, brass

FINISH: Liberon oil, wax

SETTLE
PEIDIAN CAI
ART CENTER COLLEGE OF DESIGN | INSTRUCTOR: DAVID MOCARSKI

2017
HM
HONORABLE
MENTION

What was your inspiration for this piece?

My inspiration was to create a flexible work surface for all the new work-from-home employees. This coffee table provides people with convenience and a quality work experience. The storage ideas were inspired by the divider concept in a bento box.

What were your project goals?
Did you use any unique construction methods?

My goals were to create a useful work area with multiple storage compartments. The end product includes two trays, a wireless phone charger, and an extension cord to keep the working surface clean and neat.

What challenges did you encounter?

One challenge was how to hide the extension cord in a table leg. I decided to cut the leg into two parts; one part is glued on the table, while the other is made removable with magnets. I also wanted to be able to open the storage covers without cutting holes in them. Cutting slight angles on both sides of the storage tray allow you to push the cover down to open it.

Did you use any special equipment or software?

I used Rhino and SolidWork for digital modeling.

DIMENSIONS: 14" H x 36" W x 24" D
WEIGHT: 40 lb.
MATERIALS: White oak (solid, veneer) or walnut (solid, veneer), upholstery
FINISH: Rubio Monocoat Precolor Aqua (White)

DEMILUNE SUNRISE

LUCINDA DALY

THE KRENOV SCHOOL | INSTRUCTOR: LAURA MAYS

What was your inspiration for this piece?

This entry table was inspired by the Art Deco movement, specifically the work of Emile-Jacques Ruhlmann. It does not mimic one of his works, but incorporates elements such as torpedo legs and a dropdown brass pull reminiscent of his cloth tassels.

What were your project goals?
Did you use any unique construction methods?

My project goal was to build something elegant and technically demanding. The most challenging aspects of this project were making the bent lamination for the body, creating a veneered fan-shaped pattern with a semi-circle for the top, and cutting curved dovetails on the drawer front.

What challenges did you encounter?

I was trimming the front edge of the top on the router table and it spun out, leaving a 5″ gash along the front edge of my fan-shaped veneers. The solution I came up with was to move the whole top forward 3/4″ and add a spoiler at the back. As it turns out, the pencil rail was a design element the piece really needed.

Did you use any special equipment or software?

For the bent lamination, I built an MDF form and used about thirty clamps to hold the four layers of bubinga in place. I designed a semi-circle jig with male and female parts to place the bubinga sun shape on the veneered top. I also made the dropdown pull; this was my first experience working in brass.

DIMENSIONS: 33″ H x 35″ W x 13″ D
WEIGHT: 40 lb.
MATERIALS: Bubinga, quilted maple (veneer), maple (solid, veneer), cherry, Port Orford cedar, brass

OSCILLIER

BRYCE SIMPSON

JAMES MADISON UNIVERSITY | INSTRUCTOR: SEAN YOO

2019

F

FINALIST

What was your inspiration for this piece?

My inspiration came from the book *The Little Prince*, where the prince travels to different planets. The common theme is to never lose your creative imagination as you grow. This design is based loosely on a merry-go-round and a spinning top—and what a spinning top looks like as it loses momentum.

What were your project goals? Did you use any unique construction methods?

The goal was to build something that reflected my inspiration. The lazy Susan design of the coffee table is meant to be used for entertainment for you and guests, and even for your kids.

What challenges did you encounter?

While the tapering circle design was straight forward, the difficult part was wrapping the cone shape in bendable plywood and then veneer. I couldn't use just one whole sheet since it tapers downward. To solve this, I cut the bendable plywood into triangles, resulting in less material on the bottom and more material on the top.

Did you use any special equipment or software?

I used SolidWorks 3D CAD software and a CNC router to cut the plywood. I also used a lazy Susan mechanism to create the spinning table.

DIMENSIONS: 16″ H x 32″ W x 32″ D
WEIGHT: 30 lb.
MATERIALS: Baltic birch plywood, bendable plywood, walnut (veneer)
FINISH: Wipe-on polyurethane

REULEAUX

DAVID AWERMAN

PALOMAR COLLEGE | INSTRUCTOR: CHANCE COALTER

What was your inspiration for this piece?

This project originated as an experiment with the Reuleaux Triangle, which, in geometry, is defined as a shape of constant width. I played with it on the computer until it evolved into a table.

What were your project goals?
Did you use any unique construction methods?

This piece is unique, for me, in that it's the first project I've built completely from my own design without any specific guidelines. The legs are bent to a radius but on a bias, making them look twisted. The table is rotationally symmetric, but changes shape depending on the angle from which you view it. One leg could even appear to be straight. The top has an angled waterfall edge applied with hide glue.

What challenges did you encounter?

The wood for this project was provided for me and wasn't anything like what I had in mind when designing it. This caused some challenges throughout. I had to cut my own veneer and the lychee wasn't flexible enough to yield a solid bent lamination. I decided to laminate each leg in poplar on the form, then veneer all sides with lychee. It looks possibly even better than I planned; it just took five extra steps per leg. The aluminum shelves at the base were added to stabilize the legs.

Did you use any special equipment or software?

I used SketchUp to draw the table, as well as the bending form used to make the legs. I used a CNC machine to cut the form. I used a vacuum press for the bent laminations and veneering.

DIMENSIONS: 41″ H x 24″ W x 24″ D
WEIGHT: 25 lb.
MATERIALS: Pacific Coast maple, lychee, aluminum
FINISH: Conversion varnish, paste wax

FLOATING

MATTHEW JAEHN

PALOMAR COLLEGE | INSTRUCTOR: GREG WEASE

What was your inspiration for this piece?

I wanted to design a piece with a seemingly floating top.

Did you use any unique construction methods?

The open space between the beveled lychee top and figured maple aprons and legs give the appearance the top is floating. The through tenons from the lychee supports stand proud of the maple aprons.

What challenges did you encounter?

The design challenge was to give just enough support to the top to keep it flat, yet as little as possible.

DIMENSIONS: 33″ H x 42″ W x 16″ D

WEIGHT: 35 lb.

MATERIALS: Figured lychee, figured maple

FINISH: Mohawk Conversion

Varnish, Liberon paste wax

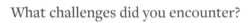

SUSPENSION TABLE

STEPHANIE LUNIESKI

CENTER FOR FURNITURE CRAFTSMANSHIP | INSTRUCTOR: ALED LEWIS

What was your inspiration for this piece?

This table originated from a sketch that I drew while studying my guitar that took on qualities of a suspension bridge. As such, every design element plays off the tension in the wires. The legs are joined at angles, as are the curved laminated stretchers. I wanted to strike a balance that suggests that the wires are pulling the legs into place while, at the same time, the legs appear to be pulling the wires taut. What I love about this table is that it takes on a unique shape from every different perspective.

What were your project goals?

The brief for this project in class was simply that we had to make a piece of furniture using lamination, steam bending, or coopering to produce a curved element. One of my goals was to create two successful laminations.

What challenges did you encounter?

The major problem I experienced was when I laminated the curved arches that connect the legs. My process left me with two curves that would not connect to the legs where I had designed them to. I took the route of increasing the size of the bend and adding more laminations to the arches, which fixed the problem and made the table sturdier. I used a system for holding signs that included tension cable (wire rope), adjustable height fittings, and screws. It was a fun challenge to figure out how to mount these materials into the table and to make it look its best.

DIMENSIONS: 31″ H x 48″ W x 16″ D
WEIGHT: 35 lb.
MATERIALS: White oak (solid, veneer), tension cable
FINISH: KemVar

BENZIE CENTRAL HIGH SCHOOL
Benzonia, MI
benziecentralhuskies.org

Instructor: Dave Barresi

Thaller, Wyatt: 2021, Queen Anne Tilt-Top Pie Crust Table, 150

CADILLAC HIGH SCHOOL
Cadillac, MI
cadillacschools.org

Instructor: Jason Stange

Stange, Maxwell: 2019, Angry Fish, 79

CEDAR RIDGE HIGH SCHOOL
Hillsborough, NC
orangecountyfirst.com/crhs

Instructor: Keith Yow

Pereeboom, Katja: 2019, Mid-Century Modern Coffee Table, 161

Pereeboom, Katja: 2019, Sinking Chair, 103

Shiplett, Matthew: 2017, Cherry blAwesome, 154

CORNER CANYON HIGH SCHOOL
Draper, UT
cchs.canyonsdistrict.org

Instructor: Timothy McNeill

Carter, Keaton: 2019, Serenity, 72

Chidester, Sadie: 2017, Everwood, 78

Edmiston, Hope: 2017, Rowan's Rocker, 106

Farnsworth, Jacob: 2021, Contemporary Table, 156

Farnsworth, Katie: 2021, Sundown, 70

Johnson, Spencer: 2017, Concepts in Parallel, 100

Johnson, Spencer: 2017, Triple Helix, 158

Johnson, Spencer: 2019, Visions of Rhythm, 152

Moon, Shane: 2017, Juney Babe, 74

Richards, Savannah: 2021, Blue Grace, 76

Zarbock, Braxton: 2019, Rosetta, 77

DAKOTA HIGH SCHOOL
Macomb, MI
chippewavalleyschools.org

Instructor: Chad Campau

Girard, Tylor: 2017, Heritage Protected, 33

Steger, Matthew: 2019, Honestly Elegant, 159

DALE JACKSON CAREER CENTER
Lewisville, TX
lisd.net/teccw

Instructor: Joseph Davis

Hassett, Kyle: 2017, Symphony of Contrast, 32

Hassett, Kyle: 2019, The Big Slick, 130

DEER PARK HIGH SCHOOL
Deer Park, WA
dphs.dpsd.org

Instructor: Kevin Kernan

Westerman, Cody: 2017, The Daddy Chair, 54

FLETCHER'S MEADOW SECONDARY SCHOOL
Brampton, ON, Canada
peelschools.org

Instructor: Peter Boeckh

Mawalal, Elizabeth: 2017, Aurora, 59

FRANKFORT HIGH SCHOOL
Frankfort, MI
frankfort.k12.mi.us

Instructor: David Barresi

Ness, Ethan: 2019, Super Scoot, 52

Reznich, Jack: 2019, Super Scoot, 52

Tondu, Andrew: 2021, Shaker Bedside Table, 128

FREMONT HIGH SCHOOL
Fremont, MI
fremont.net/schools/hs

Instructor: Rick Tank

Visscher, Garrett: 2019, Zig-Zag Corner Cabinet TV Stand, 31

LINCOLN EAST HIGH SCHOOL
Lincoln, NE
ehs.lps.org

Instructors: Jon Heithold, Jeffrey McCabe

Al-Yaseen, Mohammed: 2021, Some Assembly Required, 56

Al-Yaseen, Mohammed: 2021, The Nest, 96

Davis, Caidell: 2019, The Limbert, 105

Miles, Josiah: 2021, Lumbarest, 50

Miller, Logan: 2019, L. & J.G. Stickley Prairie Chair, 98

MARK KEPPEL HIGH SCHOOL
Alhambra, CA
mkhs.org

Instructor: Cuong Lam

Wong, Ashley: 2021, Outdoor Furniture, 134

MUSTANG HIGH SCHOOL
Mustang, OK
mustangps.org

Instructor: Mike McGarry

Bruce, Baylor: 2017, Dimensions, 162

Holt, Zack: 2019, Zarycha Safari, 157

Weidner, Kailan: 2019, Oops! I Broke It., 26

NEWBERG SENIOR HIGH SCHOOL
Newberg, OR
newberg.k12.or.us/nhs

Instructor: Rob Lewis

Sarkisian, Roehben: 2017, Quarter-Scale Mud Wagon, 80

PRINCETON DAY SCHOOL
Princeton, NJ
pds.org

Instructor: Chris Maher

Emann, Walter: 2017, Chikuu tou Sora, 136

Emann, Walter: 2019, The Klein Table, 160

Gerschel, Giulia: 2017, DoDici, 132

Klein, Christopher: 2017, A Rock in the Right Direction, 104

REED-CUSTER HIGH SCHOOL
Braidwood, IL
rc255.net/RCHS

Instructor: Mark Smith

Norton, Chandler: 2019, Riot Arts Gaming Chair, 58

ROLLA TECHNICAL INSTITUTE
Rolla, MO
rtirtc.rolla31.org

Instructor: Robert Studdard

Daniels, Cole: 2019, Hard Ninety, 135

Keeney, Tyler: 2019, Treble, 81

Kelley, Dakota: 2021, Juke Box, 24

Studdard, Zach: 2017, Doble Placer, 107

SAINT CROIX CENTRAL HIGH SCHOOL
Hammond, WI
scc.k12.wi.us

Instructor: Garret Wenzel

Olson, David: 2021, Adirondack Chair, 102

SAN JACINTO HIGH SCHOOL
San Jacinto, CA
sjhs.sanjacinto.k12.ca.us

Instructor: Roy Castillo

Cantu Pirelli, Fernando: 2021, Walnut Entertainment Credenza, 30

WEST JORDAN HIGH SCHOOL
West Jordan, UT
westjordanhigh.org

Instructor: Richard Minor Jr.

Provard, Sarah: 2017, Musically Inclined, 28

SCHOOL DIRECTORY POST-SECONDARY

ART CENTER COLLEGE OF DESIGN
Pasadena, CA
artcenter.edu

Instructors: David Mocarski, John Ford, Penny Herscovitch

Cai, Peidian: 2017, Settle, 176

Fan, Chenchen: 2017, Lavida, 124

Xiong, Jialun: 2017, Canvas, 147

AUBURN UNIVERSITY
Auburn, AL
auburn.edu

Instructor: Tin-Man Lau

Xue, Haoran: 2017, Diad, 93

BRIGHAM YOUNG UNIVERSITY
Provo, UT
byu.edu

Instructor: Timothy McNeill

Tirrell, Ryan: 2019, Game Table, 146

CALIFORNIA COLLEGE OF THE ARTS
Oakland, CA
cca.edu

Instructor: Russell Baldon

Alt, Valerie: 2019, Detach, 140

CENTER FOR FURNITURE CRAFTSMANSHIP
Rockport, ME
woodschool.org

Instructors: Aled Lewis, Tim Rousseau

Appelbaum, Dotan: 2021, Abulafia Lectern, 82

Boyle, Evan: 2017, Pua Side Table, 62

Brown, Joe: 2017, Ash Cabinet, 38

Gordon, Glen: 2021, Arches Sideboard, 40

Kim, Jinsoo: 2021, Flying Table, 164

Kim, Jinsoo: 2021, Sideboard with a Void, 34

Lohn, Alexander: 2019, Maritza's Bench, 115

Lunieski, Stephanie: 2017, Suspension Table, 181

Merchant, Christopher: 2019, Cabinet End Table, 36

Merchant, Christopher: 2019, Convex Desk, 172

Sassa, Osamu: 2019, Artist's Desk, 64

Sassa, Osamu: 2019, Coopered Daybed, 110

Scully, Claire: 2017, Wave, 90

Willmon, Tyler: 2019, Mt. Rockvale Stool, 122

Willmon, Tyler: 2019, Mt. Rockvale Vanity, 45

EDINBORO UNIVERSITY
Edinboro, PA
edinboro.edu

Instructor: Karen Ernst

Zimmerman, Ryan: 2017, Modular Stools, 125

HAYWOOD COMMUNITY COLLEGE
Clyde, NC
haywood.edu

Instructor: Brian Wurst

Tolini, Alexander: 2019, Chest of Drawers, 44

HERRON SCHOOL OF ART AND DESIGN
Indianapolis, IN
herron.iupui.edu

Instructor: Katie Hudnall

Slightom, Sarah: 2019, Diamond Lamp, 92

IOWA STATE UNIVERSITY
Ames, IA
iastate.edu

Instructor: Matthew Obbink

Christianson, Samuel: 2019, 72.5 Chair, 60

Miklo, Nathan: 2019, 72.5 Chair, 60

JAMES MADISON UNIVERSITY
Harrisonburg, VA
jmu.edu

Instructors: Kevin Phaup, Sean Yoo

Duong, Hung: 2019, Mariposa Convertible Table, 66

Simpson, Bryce: 2019, Oscillier, 178

MADISON COLLEGE
Madison, WI
madisoncollege.edu

Instructor: Patrick Molzahn

Hefferan, Jenny: 2021, Nested Console Tables, 138

NORTH BENNET STREET SCHOOL
Boston, MA
nbss.edu

Instructor: Dan Faia

Osach, Daniel: 2021, Joined Arts & Crafts Chair in Walnut & Leather, 114

Ouyang, Zala: 2019, Mahogany Music Stand, 84

Ouyang, Zala: 2019, Walnut Jewelry Cabinet, 42

Thibeault, Joseph: 2021, Queen Anne Chair, 117

Tobin, Avrom: 2021, Harp Back Chair, 108

PALOMAR COLLEGE
San Marcos, CA
palomar.edu

Instructors: Jennifer Anderson, Jerry Beaudry, Chance Coalter, Jack Stone, Greg Wease

Awerman, David: 2017, Reuleaux, 179

Carter, Steven: 2019, Low-Back Chair, 120

Jaehn, Matthew: 2017, Floating, 180

Kolb, Farron: 2017, Maloof-Style Rocker, 116

McCravy, Ed: 2017, Gibson f-5 Mandolin, 86

Strenger, William: 2017, Scythe, 142

Zubieta, George (Randy): 2017, Linda, 67

PITTSBURG STATE UNIVERSITY
Pittsburg, KS
pittstate.edu

Instructor: Jordan Backs, Charlie Phillips

Galliart, Sam: 2019, Stuffed Sapele, 118

Spahr, Zachary: 2019, Coupe de Ville Mid-Century Modern Bed, 89

SEATTLE CENTRAL COLLEGE
Seattle, WA
seattlecentral.edu

Instructor: Jeffrey Wasserman

Campanie, Cody: 2017, Azulejos Table, 168

Miller, Richard: 2019, Oblio Chair, 121

SELKIRK COLLEGE
Nelson, BC, Canada
selkirk.ca

Instructor: David Ringheim, Scott Stevens

Belliveau-Thompson, Shaun: 2021, The Truman Table, 174

Carr, Aleasha: 2021, Zig-Zag Stardust Coffee Table, 170

Nelson, Madelaine: 2021, And the Rabbit Jumped Over the Moon, 144

Stevens, Scott: 2017, Writing Table, 173

Strom, Erica: 2017, Rosewood Entertainment Stand, 47

SUNY BUFFALO STATE COLLEGE
Buffalo, NY
suny.buffalostate.edu

Instructor: Sunhwa Kim

Koloski, Susan: 2021, Revolution Mirror, 88

THE FURNITURE INSTITUTE OF MASSACHUSETTS
Beverly, MA

Instructor: Philip C. Lowe

Maraldo, Nicholas: 2019, Nautical Marquetry Table, 166

McDonald, Derek: 2017, Hibiscus Flowers in Bloom, 91

THE KRENOV SCHOOL
Fort Bragg, CA
thekrenovschool.org

Instructor: Laura Mays

Daly, Lucinda: 2019, Demilune Sunrise, 177

Giovingo, Matt: 2017, Li'l Dipper, 43

Nelson, Scott: 2019, Recidivus, 119

Sterns, Joshua: 2017, Cherry Bowfront Cabinet, 46

Sterns, Joshua: 2019, Cuban Mahogany Night Stands, 175

Wong, Maggi: 2017, C.S. Wong, 112

UNIVERSITY OF IDAHO
Moscow, ID
uidaho.edu

Instructor: Jay Pengilly

Albertson, Erica: 2017, The Lost Call, 123

UNIVERSITY OF KENTUCKY
Lexington, KY
uky.edu

Instructor: Michael Jacobs

Westfall, Chris: 2017, 5-Day Valet, 65

STUDENT INDEX

LEVEL INDEX HIGH SCHOOL

Text and photography © 2022

Publisher: Paul McGahren
Editorial Director: Kerri Grzybicki
Design & Layout: Robert Schehl
Photographer: Alan Harp
AWFS® Association Director: Adria Salvatore
AWFS® Education Director: Adam Kessler

Cedar Lane Press
PO Box 5424
Lancaster, PA 17606-5424

Paperback ISBN: 978-1-950934-90-4
ePub ISBN: 978-1-950934-91-1

Library of Congress Control Number: 2022934622

Printed in the United States of America
10 9 8 7 6 5 4 3 2 1

Projects shown on covers listed clockwise from top left:
Front cover: Concepts in Parallel by Spencer Johnson, p. 100; Reuleaux by David Awerman, p. 179; Revolution Mirror by Susan Koloski, p. 88; Diamond Lamp by Sarah Slightom, p. 92; Zarycha Safari by Zack Holt, p. 157; Zig-Zag Stardust Coffee Table by Aleasha Carr, p. 170.

Back cover: Sideboard with a Void by Jinsoo Kim, p. 34; Harp Back Chair by Avrom Tobin, p. 108; Juney Babe by Shane Moon, p. 74; Jukebox by Dakota Kelley, p. 24; Chikuu Tou Sora by Walter Emann, p. 136.

Note: The following list contains names used in *Fresh Wood Design Book* that may be registered with the United States Copyright Office:

Abalam; Adobe (Photoshop); ALPHACAM; Apple (iPhone 4S); ApplePly; Arbortech; AutoCAD; AWFS®; AWFS®Fair; Bendy Ply; Blender; Bluetooth; BobCAD-CAM; Cadillac (Coupe deVille); Chemcraft; CHIMEI (POLYLAC); Dremel; EMTECH (EM6000); EnRoute; Epifanes; Europly; Ferrari (F430); Festool (DOMINO); Fusion 360; General Finishes (Arm-R-Seal, Gel Topcoat); GlenTek (Warthog); Homag; KerfKore; KeyShot; King Arthur's Tools (Holey Galahad); Laguna Tools; Liberon (Black Bison Wax Polish, Finishing Oil); Mahoney's Finishes; Masonite; MasterCAM; Metropolitan Museum of Art; Minwax (Formby's Furniture Workshop, Polycrylic); ML Campbell (Magnalac, MagnaMax); Mod Podge; Mohawk Conversion Varnish; Old-Fashioned Milk Paint Co.; Onsrud; Opendesk; Osmo (Oil Stain, Polyx-Oil, TopOil, Wood Wax Finish); Pinterest; Pollmeier (BauBuche); Rhino; Rubio (Monocoat Precolor Aqua); SeedLac; Sharpie; Sher-Wood (KemVar); SketchUp; Skidmore's Liquid Beeswax Woodfinish; SolidWorks; SOLO; SOSS; Sutherland Welles Ltd. (Murdoch's Hard Oil, Murdoch's Hard Sealer); *The Art of Japanese Joinery*; *The Little Prince*; Thermwood; Timber Products Company (GreenT Pro-Core); Unique Machine; Universal Laser; VacuPress; Varathane Wood Stain; Vectric (Aspire, VCarve); Virutex; Watco; Weeke; Wilsonart; woodWOP

To learn more about Cedar Lane Press books, or to find a retailer near you, email info@cedarlanepress.com or visit us at www.cedarlanepress.com.

AWFS® RESOURCES

YOUWOOD.COM

A new website to showcase careers in the wood industry, geared toward students and job seekers. Find career profiles, spotlights of wood industry professionals, articles, videos, industry events, and more! The YouWood campaign and website are produced by the Wood Industry Resource Collaborative (WIRC), a coalition of industry associations, of which AWFS® is a founding and leading member.

WOODINDUSTRYED.ORG

A searchable database of woodworking and related schools and training programs. Has over 1,000 schools listed from throughout North America. Search by geographical filters or type of program, certification, etc. Also includes listings of trade associations, trade press, industry events, career resources, and other information for students, educators, job seekers, and industry partners.

"MEET THE NEW FACE OF MANUFACTURING"

AWFS® initiative to improve the perception of the wood products manufacturing industry as offering desirable, creative, and fun opportunities. Highlights young professionals in various career paths. Free posters and videos. Contact AWFS/Adria Salvatore adria@awfs.org or (323) 215-0311 to request posters; go to YouTube.com/AWFSFair to see the videos.

CUE CAREER
CueCareer.com

A website that connects students with "overlooked" industries and career paths, and the associations that represent them. Check out industry profile interview videos and more information about the wood industry (and all industry sectors) on this website. (Find wood industry videos and resources under "manufacturing" and look for the AWFS® page.)

MFG DAY
MFGDay.com

Manufacturing Day is an opportunity to showcase our industry and careers to educate students about manufacturing and how integral it is to the local, national, and global economy. National MFG Day is the first Friday of October. Go to the website to learn more about hosting an event or finding events to attend.

SKILLSUSA
SkillsUSA.org; SkillsUSACA.org

AWFS® and the Society of Wood Manufacturing develop, organize, and run the SkillsUSA California region 3 and 6 and state Cabinetmaking and Introductory Woodworking student contests. With over 300,000 student, educator, and industry members, SkillsUSA is one of the largest national career technical student organizations and is a partnership of students, teachers, and industry working together to ensure America has a skilled workforce. California is currently one of the largest and fastest-growing state organizations—connect today!

SOCIETY OF WOOD MANUFACTURING (SWM)
AWFS.org/education/swm

AWFS® launched this Southern California chapter to connect industry with education. Active SWM members, consisting of high school and college educators and industry professionals, meet monthly to identify ways to work together. The SWM group runs the SkillsUSA CA regional and state woodworking contests; participates in MFG Day events, trade shows, and conferences; and serves on school advisory committees.

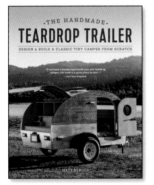

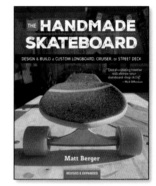
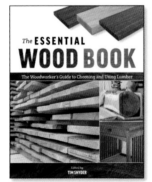